The Light of My Life

God & D. Howard

Original writing 1995, Donna Marie Howard and God
This book was originally called "My Talk With God".
Added material 1996, 1997, 1998 and 1999,
channeled from God,
Written by Donna Marie Howard

Computer typed and edited by: Samantha Hagman
Carol Stewart and Dana R. Stuart
Computer assisted by: Jan and Kristen Hagman and
Shirley M. Fountain

ISBN 1-929937-00-8

Self published.
Printed in the United States of America,
September, 1999

This book is not meant to replace doctors or medication. The author of this book, directly or indirectly, does not give medical advice nor prescribes the use of any techniques as a form of treatment for medical problems. Any one attached to this book will not be held responsible for any techniques you choose to use from it.

Be on the lookout for upcoming books.

My Spiritual Journey With Babe Ruth
from the Damn Yankees back to Boston

Dennis
A true Poltergeist ghost story

It's a Cat's Life
A true story for all ages

Cat Craze
Cute Cat Pictures

If My Body Could Talk
My story of illness to obesity, then back
to health and average weight.
From Hospitals to Holistic Healings

Spiritualist Church

HEALING AFFIDAVIT

This form may be completed by those who have received healing through a spiritual healer, whether the healing be mental, physical, or spiritual. This may refer to a single visit to the healer's chair, several visits, or absentee healing.

Thank you

Name of Spiritual Healer: Donna M. Howard
Name of Person Receiving Healing: Jonathan Mittell
Address: Healing took place at Donna's home.
Dates of Healing: May 1995 through May 1996.
Specific Health Condition: Late night binge eating, feelings of despair - thinking, "There must be something evil within me that takes control of my desires."
Any Feelings or Sensations received during the healing: Feeling of clearing in the chest - feeling lighter and freer. Feeling I no longer have something evil within me, which I have to hide and keep from the world.
Results of Healings: I feel I have the power of decision to reach out to human contact, and if I want to eat at night, even more than my thinking mind says is enough, I still love myself and approve of who I am.

Donna and I met at a Spiritualist Church. We were attracted to each others' energy and interests. I was attracted to her power to pierce directly through my own energies, keeping me from going through my pain.

Written Permission given by: Jonathan B. Mittell
on May 27, 1996 and again on January 24, 1999.

Jonathan thank you so much for sharing your soul, and lessons with all of us. God be with you!

Spiritualist Church

HEALING AFFIDAVIT

This form may be completed by those who have received healing through a spiritual healer, whether the healing be mental, physical, or spiritual. This may refer to a single visit to the healer's chair, several visits, or absentee healing.

Thank you

Name of Spiritual Healer: Donna Howard
Name of Person/Animal receiving healing: Dempsey at Mulberry (Boxer dog)
Date(s) of healing: 2/24/98 and continuing
Specific condition healed: Dempsey has an Anaplastic Sarcoma - a non-operable aggressive tumor on his face.
Any feelings or sensations received during healing: It has given us all a feeling of well-being hope. When I had done the hands-on healing with the group at the church, I felt a great welling sensation coming from my heart and spreading to Demps.
Results of healings: Since seeking Donna's help, the tumor has reduced some in size. Dempsey has gained back energy and appetite. Also, as a result of Donna's help, we are bringing him to the church on Sundays for healing. Donna also got me into researching homeopathic remedies, which I believe to be a big help. Right from the first phone call to Donna, we all felt so much more at peace. This is a very painful time in our lives, and to know how many people have touched our lives through Donna's caring is a miracle in itself.
Notarized March 17, 1998.

The views and opinions expressed in this book are those of the author and not intended to reflect on the philosophy of these churches, nor do the views and opinions of these Churches necessarily reflect Donna Howard's views and opinions.

Thank you so much for sharing this touching story with all of us, God bless!

January 18, 1999

Dear Donna,

You're a dear and treasured friend.

Thank you so much for helping me to get my story out to the public in hopes of finding my twin brother.

Thank you also for helping my sister Karin and her family to sell their two family house which had been on the market quite a few times over a five year period, to no avail. The fact is that strange occurrences had been going on in her home for the twenty five years that she lived there. One occurrence was, a very heavy sticky door was mysteriously opening, whenever my sister walked from one room into another with a pile of clean, folded baby clothes in her arms. Among other things, shades were going up and down on their own and stopping when told to.

Karin and her family found old letters in their attic from Sweden. That, along with the strange occurrences prompted them to go to town hall to find out who had lived there before them. They found that a four year old boy and his father, who had been an ambassador to Sweden, had both died in this home many years before. I know you had no way of knowing this. Yet, at the cleansing you mentioned some of these things, while talking him and his son into going over to the other side.

As you know, while we were praying, another ghost named Mary, who lived across the street, ran past you home to the light. What you didn't know is: later, Karin found out from Mary's son that his dishes were no longer mysteriously being washed at night.

Oh, I almost forgot to tell you about a funny incident that happened there one day, about three years before your cleansing. While my sister and grown niece were sitting in the family room watching television together, a toy fire engine, which had been sitting on the floor in front of the toy box, started up and moved around the room on its own! This toy had a switch that needed to be turned on. Not only that, but the fire bell also started clanging loudly, even though another switch was needed to turn the bell on! These two adults just sat there and laughed in amazement the whole while, assuming it was the little boy's spirit who was playing with it. I guess the three of them had a fun time!

The house sold within a week after your spiritual cleansing.

Thanks again for all you have done and for all the fun "experiences" throughout our lives.

Love,
Samantha

Dear Samantha and Jan,

Jan, it's funny how you came all the way from Sweden to Boston, just to meet Sam and get married. When I look at both of you, it seems like you were "always" together and meant to be since BEFORE BIRTH. On the same token, I feel like I was born to be on the road that I am on, and for the past few months I have realized that both of you are on that same road with me.

Samantha, I am SO HONORED that you, a good friend for so many years, said that I have talent and laughed in all the right places while reading "The Light Of My Life." Sam, you were the first to look it over, and remember I'm not used to hearing positive things from people who are close to me.

I want to thank both of you, and your son Glenn, for praying with me, as well as others, for the Red Sox in "1997 & 1998." In the future we will continue to pray, in hopes of releasing eighty years of negativity which was wished onto them. In that way we prove that PRAYER really DOES work.

It's strange how in April of "99" while copying the pages of this book, pages 14 & 22 were missing. Ironically your birthday is April 14th and mine is April 22nd.

We have had some interesting times together, may we have many more. If it wasn't for both of you this book would still be unfinished. "Thank you," falls short for ALL you both have done, you are truly earth angels.

Sam and Jan, I love you both.
Your friend forever.
Love,
Donna

Donna Marie Howard is one of the most remarkable young women of our era. Donna is an exciting and multi-faceted personality. There is a side of Donna Marie Howard that is a compassionate and powerful spiritualist capable of healing a troubled mind, body, and soul. Then there is the charming, well-mannered, and very feminine Lady Donna that can change your heart. And there is Miss Howard who is the ultimate champion of our much-endangered wildlife and much abused domestic pets. Don't harm an animal in the presence of Miss Donna Marie Howard or else you will see the Lady turn into a tiger.

Donna Howard has the power to mend a world broken by crime and terror. If the world would read her words and put them into action, then there would be a chance to save this planet from self-imposed destruction.

Donna Marie is here for everyone!

Hank A. Pasquerella
B.S. Ed., Salem State College
M.A., Suffolk University
M. Ed., Tufts University

Certifications: History
Geography
English
Psychology
Philosophy

Written: 9/28/95

Preface

I asked who was speaking to me. My answer was "*God*." Everything in this book including the title, size and color was channeled from God through me to write down. *I can't change anything*! Even *my* questions and statements flowed very quickly through my head and hand which is called automatic writing. My messages come to me as if you KNOW who is on the other end of the phone *before* you pick it up. Visions and conversations of my life, along with directions, would come to me over and over again until finally I would insert them into the proper chapters. Then, and ONLY *then,* would they leave my head, (only positive, no negative). Most of the dictated writings without dates are from "1995."

I was led to believe this book was to be printed and distributed in 1995 but circumstances beyond MY control prevented it. As it turned out, more needed to be added to it in 1996, 1997, 1998 and finally 1999, similar to a diary.

You should read this book more than once to be able to absorb it all. Open daily to any page for a message.

Remember to relax, even if things don't go your way *there is a reason for* EVERYTHING. "There are NO *coincidences* or accidents in life."

The original writing of this book was finished within seven days and nights. If you have *any* doubts whether I could do this book *without God*, just ask *any* of my former teachers. You see, I have a learning disability called Attention Deficit Disorder. Please understand that having A.D.D. doesn't automatically mean that you are stupid or disruptive.

October 27, 1996
The Light of My Life

The Light of My Life

We are born with NO WALLS to hold us back from our Spiritual knowledge. Yet as we grow a little older, society and we start to create and build our walls thicker and taller.

Finally, the now deep, overweight, secretive, rugged wall suffocates, surrounds and encases us sleepily in it.

Sometimes I felt as if I was walking down a long, endless, dark hallway. Then a little twinkling light would start shimmering at the very end of the now dimly lit hall, but when I finally came close to the light, IT would quickly disappear.

You *will* learn in "The Light of My Life" a simple way, through interesting true stories of my life and others, how to become *aware* and *AWAKE* and for answers to *WHY* and what's *IT ALL* about?? You will *get IT* in this book. You will finally know how to stop your own negative circles and learn how to break down your *dense walls* that have been keeping you from knowing some secrets of *THE UNIVERSE.*

This book is about healing, relationships, children, friends, family, you, poetry, plants, pictures, animals, anorexia, alcoholics, Alzheimer's, A.D.D., love, laughter, God, Satan, people, ghosts (spirits/souls) in this world and beyond, and much, much more.

Walk with me on my Spiritual road and learn through these captivating stories how to be whole! I'm sure at least one of these stories will trigger a familiar memory in you.

The darkest hour is just before *DAWN.*

Only *YOU* can make this change in me. Only *YOU, YOU ARE MY DESTINY.*

I am self publishing, so after expenses, contributions from this book will go to homeless kids and cats.

Thank you,
Donna Marie Howard,
Cats and Kids

BOOK BLESSING

The Book of Love

Protect me and all others who read and harbor*
this book of knowledge and love.

To let them see the truth and help themselves
to *learn* and *care* forever more.
Thank you, God.

Saint Michael the Archangel

Saint Michael the Archangel
"Defend us in battle."
Be our protector against the wickedness and snares of the devil.

May God rebuke him; we humbly pray;
And do Thou, *O Prince* of the heavenly host,
By the *Power* of God, thrust into hell, Satan and *all* evil spirits
Who wander through the world for the ruin of souls.
Amen.

Thank you God, and Saint Michael, for everything.
Donna Marie

Harbor: Was used as a verb meaning to provide with a usually temporary place to live.

Earth Possessions

On my walk this morning
I noticed yet
Another beautiful stone
That I would love to take home.

But I am always told
To hold it for a while
Then let it go
With a smile.

God said to me,
"Donna, Let IT be
Then you'll be free
For ETERNITY.

You have enough
In your home
So I'm asking you
To leave it alone."

Once I picked one up
HE said, "Put IT back
Just enjoy it FOR A TIME,
THEN
LEAVE IT BEHIND.

You see THAT'S
What life's all about
Having
Then
Giving OUT.

Having a LOT of THINGS is bad
And leaving them behind is sad.
To think we might not be that smart
INSTEAD – to fill our EMPTY heart.

The Indian had a small teepee
Because you see – HIS world ***was*** *FREE*

I love you ALL
You know that
But I'm asking you
Just put it back."

God and Donna
Saturday, October 26, 1996, 10:00 A.M.

To all of my pets here and out of sight, the nameless ones from childhood, and Marco, Tabby, YoYo, Bartet, Angel, Ramses, and my stray cat Blackie.

Destiny

I walked past
A lot of cats.

Till I met you,
Now we are two.

You're meant to be
You see, with me.

When we're apart,
You're in my heart.

Till the end of time
You see...you're mine.

God and Donna

Written by Donna Marie Howard from God,

Monday, October 28, 1996, 7:45 AM

To All The Children: Love

I saw some kids
Picking on a cat.
I said to them,
"Please don't do *that.*"

They frowned and said,
"We'll go to bed
For being bad
And getting *God* mad."

They said to ME,
"We'll set it free,
And don't despair,
The cat's *all right*,
He ran from us
Clear out of sight."

"Here's your *heart,*
Promise not to harm
ANY animal from *NOW on.*

At HEAVEN'S door
You'll promise, '*Nevermore,*'
But by then
You've *already* sinned!"

"PLEASE DON'T DO THAT!" – GOD

October 28, 1996, 7:30 AM

Chapter 1

My Prayer to God

I discovered my childhood has been following me around *everywhere* I go. I would like to share my stories with you in the hope that you might see something that will teach you about *your own* CIRCLES in life. Let's learn and clear up the past so we can *go forward* with a *clear* and *clean* slate.

If you really want to search into your soul, pray, meditate and even take a sabbatical for your *full* lessons to come to be. If you find that you're not able to sleep for a few nights, for one reason or another after your prayers, you will know that *this* is your opportunity to learn. Be careful what you pray for, you just might get it.

Say these prayers as you read and don't be afraid to just LET GO. Whatever *your* own prayer is that might come to you, is perfect for YOU and GOD.

My prayer to God:

I need to know how to find what it is that I have been missing all these painful years. Show me, please show me, I'm ready now. I don't care WHAT *it takes. I have been suffering too long.* PLEASE *get it over with.*

Since that prayer, I have been kept awake for quite a few nights and as a result of that a part of my brain has been awakened. I can see everything more clearly now. *In my awakened state* my everyday occurrences have taken on new meaning. My sleep deprivation has created a clarity that people fast for days to achieve. I see it *all* now. There really are *no coincidences*. Here are some examples:

Jake

My mother (in her late eighties) was in the hospital after once again falling. She told me of another time when she had fallen down the narrow, old cellar steps and hit the rock foundation with her head, and was not able to move for quite awhile. My mother then called to Mother Mary and promised: if YOU help me I will NEVER come down these stairs again. My mother then got up, walked up the stairs, and except for some awful looking bruises, she was fine! Her stubbornness caused her to break her promise to our Mother Mary. This time, to slow her down, my mother broke her hip. She had never had an operation in her life and hadn't even been to a hospital since I was born. The doctor said it didn't look good for her. You see, she had lain on the floor for many hours with my nephew's dog, Jake, next to her the whole time. When my nephew came home from work, the Golden Retriever barked feverishly at him as if to say, "Where have you been?" Within a week of that bad experience, Jake became very sick for fear of losing my mother. His physical health improved after he received medical attention from the vet Both the dog and my nephew were very attached to my mother and took very good care of her.

I went to visit my mother around 6 P.M. while she was in the geriatric unit of the hospital. As I was standing at the foot of her bed, an aide was helping my mother lie down. This was done too fast, my mother's head hit the pillow so hard she suddenly went into a fog-like state with her eyes partially opened in ecstasy, which I have seen her go into before.

In a distant, soft voice my mother said, "I'm not ready to go yet."

Then mom answered, "Yes.. okay.. yes!"

In very slow motion, she was nodding her head up and down, as she continued to answer, "Yes!"

After a few minutes she slowly came out of the trance. While she was still in a daze I asked her, "Who were you talking to?"

"*God,*" she answered softly.
I asked, "What did He say?"
She answered, "That I'm going to be all right."
"Anything else?" I asked.
"He's going to make me better," she said.
"Is that all?" I asked. I knew there was more.
Suddenly, in her "loud Irish whisper," she bellowed,
"WHO WANTS TO KNOW?"
She was *back* with us from her trance, and I slept
better from then on knowing God was with her.

To her doctors' amazement my mother recovered but she was moved from the hospital directly into a nursing home. The four-year-old Retriever was literally heart broken. Now he was left *alone* all day long, and saddened beyond belief. He missed the snacks my mother used to throw to him. That had all changed when my mother left and Jake must have wondered, "Why am I being punished?" Within about a month of her unwillingly leaving him, he was dead. My whole family was devastated, the only thing that we ALL ever agreed on was that Jake was a wonderful dog and took very good care of my mother. He was a working dog, always protecting her. They kept each other company most of the time. It would have been nice if there had been someone for him (and other working animals) to play and exercise with during the day, to give him a break, while everyone else was at work. Instead, we had lovingly imprisoned his life with a sometimes stressful responsibility. Not that he had ever complained. It was as if he knew why he was here... another angel sent from God and his job was done.

Maggie

Just recently an acquaintance of mine, who had never heard the story about Jake, bought a Golden Retriever which her husband named Maggie. They already had a cat named Peggy, which is my niece's name. Both names are nicknames for Margaret, which is my mother's name. This girl had a son named Paul, and she had wanted to name her second son, Adam. Out of all men's names, those two are my favorites. They have *always* been my favorites, although my friend did not know that. Coincidences??...Maybe not!! But there was definitely a connection coming from somewhere and sometime.

Their Golden Retriever, Maggie, was locked in a cage alone, bored and sad, ALL day long. That was really cruel and not fair to poor Maggie. Luckily, my friend was sensitive enough to realize this injustice, and putting her family's feelings aside, she sold Maggie to a nice middle-aged man. Of course she had gone to his home a few times to make sure that he was not buying Maggie just to sell her to an experimental laboratory, or to just throw her outside in the yard. From the moment the man walked in her door, Maggie would not leave his side. His older daughter also had a dog and was willing to take Maggie if her father had to leave home overnight. Maggie would have yet another loving home to go to with a companion there for her to play with all day, while her new master was away. Maggie loved her new happy home. She and her new owner were together all the time, keeping each other company and going for a lot of walks and rides. Maggie sat right in the front seat of the truck with her new caring friend, and they shared snacks together all during the day. They protected and took good care of one another. Maggie wouldn't feel punished by being imprisoned anymore. She would *never* be alone or sad again.

In retrospect, Jake, Maggie, and my mother's life's journey had a lot in common. In a simplistic way all three are examples of how to break away from the negative circles you have been in, and show you how to look at your own similarities and connections in life. Names, places, and experiences direct our attention to the truths about who we are, where we're going, and, in this manner, we go forward using the knowledge that's around us on a day-to-day basis. By the end of this book, you will see the reflection from the mirror of your own life. You will understand how to look at it, decipher it, put it where it belongs, learn from it, and go forward. Remember, there are no coincidences.

I've finally figured out why my mother is still hanging on in a nursing home at the age of ninety-one: To see *ME whole as well as HERSELF*. She's a VERY *powerful* woman, and she will help me from the other side some day. I'm sure I will feel her spirit in church when she passes. Once I asked her to pray for a friend of mine who was very sick. She asked, "Does he want to *live,* or does he want to *die*?"

Good-bye *for now,* Mom.

Chapter 2

Life's New Story

These *short stories* were interjected - late 1997. This long chapter has a lot of very important lessons in it.

I had moved to my third house which was on Adams Street in Dorchester (pronounced in Boston as Do'chesta, as car is to ca) when I was about eleven years old, and met a new group of friends with pretty much the same type of personalities as my last group of friends. Let me introduce you to a little piece of my life. I had the pleasure of growing up with a girl who was full of life, energy, love, and who *appeared* to be happy. Christina taught me a lot of life's lessons. She knew how to turn a bad situation into a good one. She made sad people happy because she felt, "life is too short!"

Christina is about 115 pounds, 5'5", nice figure, sharp dresser, great dancer, and a wonderful person. Christina is Portuguese and Irish, she has pretty, dark-brown street-eyes, and long, curly, dark-brown hair. Christina is like a sister to me, she watched over me like a guardian angel here on Earth. I was so naive and didn't realize until many years later that she had been protecting me since we met at the "Woodie," which was the nickname for Woodrow Wilson Jr. High School, in Dorchester, Massachusetts. Believe it or not, I was quiet, timid and bashful back then. I didn't want people to notice me because I was basically insecure. As a result, I was known as: "Where's Christina's friend... what's-her-name?" She was one of my oldest and best friends - not to take away from my other GOOD friends, it was just that we hung around together a lot more. There were a lot of nights that I didn't want to go out, but Christina would call and convince me that we would be home early, and promised that *this* time she would be on time to meet me. She wanted to see if so-and-so was at Sportsman's Bar - where some of my long time treasured friends with some interesting nicknames, hung out. "Sporties" at times could be so dangerous that everyone ran from the bar and pool table area into the *ladies* room when trouble started. If all the men got there first the ladies were out of luck. Although some of the guys DID stay behind to fight, others were chased in one door of the ladies room and out the other, ending up at the back of the restaurant, unless they were unlucky enough to have someone waiting for them outside of the second ladies room door. It was every man and woman for themselves!!

One day, many years ago, in front of "Sporties" a guy named Ski, who had a REAL MEAN STREAK, was shot FIVE times. Ski got up and chased the person he knew down the street 'til he finally fell to the ground. A police officer friend of ours, along with another officer, got a radio call saying that someone was shot. They rushed to the scene and put Ski in the back of their patrol car.

On the way to the hospital our friend kept asking him, "Who did it?"

Ski would not answer.

In the hospital room the two cops, with the doctor present, asked again, "Who shot you?"

Ski finally said to the doctor, "Get rid of these guys and I'll tell YOU who did it!"

The doctor came out of the room and asked if there was a sergeant or a supervisor he could call?

Our friend asked, "Why, did he say who did it?"

The doctor answered, "Yes, a COP shot him."

He said, "A COP ! .. WHO ??"

The doctor answered, "Jay Greene!"

Our friend said, "I 'AM' Jay Greene !!"

The shooter was never found. Ski and Jay would run into one another while walking at Castle Island in "Southie" (South Boston), and every time Ski would laughingly tell that story to everyone they met. The doctor was the only one who didn't know that Jay Greene never shot Ski.

I wouldn't change a thing except to tell all of my friends how much they mean to me, how much I miss them and those fun, exciting days. Especially our friend Rainie's parties, where we always had happy times and a lot of great food. I wouldn't even change most of the hard times from those days.

Sometimes due to the other person's BAD karma and lessons we must keep on walking, and sometimes to prevent bad karma from coming back on us, we have to help, whoever and whatever! Ask your good angel for the right thing to do, and you will FEEL what should be done. Usually if you feel guilty, you've done wrong. There are cultures who don't even step on ants for fear of what goes around comes around. Where I live, some insensitive cruel people for years, have been stepping on our poor little snails whose only goal is to reach the beach, now this year we have so few. Unfortunately EVERYONE pays the price for your ignorance. I use a Kleenex to move the snails off the road, in the direction they're heading. If you laughingly say these things are insignificant, or you intentionally step on them, then you have flunked your test from God.

One evening, Christina and I went to the Continental Lounge to see if the band *Everett and The Screamers* were playing. I had a mad crush on Everett - a lot of girls did. He would look right through me when he sang these two songs, "Can't Take My Eyes Off Of You" and "You Don't Know Me." That made my whole night, and I will ALWAYS think of him whenever I hear those songs. I can STILL picture him and his band, the exact way they looked.

About ten years later, some new friends took me to a club, almost an hour's drive from home, for my birthday. All the way there I was complaining to myself that I didn't want to go that far. The four of us entered the restaurant and sat at the bar. While we were sipping Champagne and eating birthday cake (of course there was a designated driver) I glanced up at the stage, only to see Everett preparing to sing. I couldn't believe my eyes! These friends had no idea what they had done for me. After the set was over, I went up to say, "Hi," to Everett. Would he remember me? After all, Christina wasn't with me. As it turned out, he seemed happy to see me. We sat for a couple of minutes and he confessed to me that he'd had a crush on me all those years ago. Why he chose to tell me now, and not then, I have no idea - I can only guess. That was the best birthday gift I have *ever* received in my whole life! I just can't explain the euphoric feelings that were going through me. He and I were obviously "not in the cards" back then, but at least now I have some closure on those shared loving memories. The feelings live longer this way.

To break "the circle" the next time something similar happens to me, I would treat it differently by, hopefully, not being afraid to tell him that I like him, especially if he's shy. If there's any chance we are meant to be more than just "friends," rather than just dream about it, if it's truly meant to be, I can CREATE it and not let my chance pass me by.

Back to hanging out with Christina: Once again she convinced me to go out, even though I knew I would regret it if I walked through my door at 4 A.M. and had to wake up at 6 A.M. to go to work. Then we had to make the "big decision," what to wear that night. Many times we swapped clothes. Combined, we had a complete wardrobe. Most of the time, when I "loaned" her my clothes, they would be gone forever. (Similar to my mother giving my stuff away without asking me first.) So once I *learned* my lesson, I would only loan her clothes I was bored with. Anyway, we never got home before 1 A.M. I remember one morning when I called her, I asked her mother, "Where's Christina?"

She replied, .."She's out with you!!"

When Christina and I did go out, we would dance and have fun with the aforementioned group of friends that we were very close to...like family. We watched out for one another. Christina showed me how to lighten-up and not take myself and others too seriously. I learned through watching her not to be afraid to talk and joke with people. Christina never criticized me or anyone else, so it made my life's lessons with her a lot easier.

For example, when a guy asked her, "What are you doing tonight?"

She would answer kiddingly, with a twinkle in her eye, "Why? ..What did you have in mind??"

One guy continued, "I wanted to ask you out."

Christina replied, "How does it feel to *want*?"

He replied, "Familiar!!"

She said to me, "He's smarter than he looks."

I replied, "He asked you out didn't he !!"

You could only say these things to a friend, otherwise, if it was someone who "didn't like the way you parted your hair," you could end up in a fist-fight.

If someone said something to upset her, she would say, "Your mother wears combat boots!" She would say it in such a way that no-one would be angry anymore. Everyone would begin to laugh. Much later, I realized that Christina was really giving mini-healings and exorcisms.

Together, we were afraid of nothing and no one. Two of her brothers boxed once in a while and they showed her a few moves. Christina was a *very* loving person and would *never* look for trouble, yet it was nice to know if trouble came looking for us, we'd be able to handle it.

There are some people in life who just go out looking for trouble, especially in the city. We had to be prepared at all times for anything and everything. If it gets around that you won't fight, everyone will pick on you, and/or beat you up, it's like being at the bottom of the food chain. Everyone should watch his or her own back. Just recently, a friend of mine, who is gay and white, told me he went for a walk on a dangerous street in Dorchester, near where I was born. A teenager of a different race harassed him, making threats and staring hatefully at him. Don't ever make eye contact with anyone in the city - it's like a challenge, the same as in the animal kingdom.

I said to him, "You were crazy to be walking down that street."

He said, "It was broad daylight!"

I said, "Don't ever do that again! You could have been killed!"

He said he had chills up and down his spine while the teenager stalked him, but he went on to say, "It's not safe to walk anywhere!"

I replied, "We all have choices in this life. That was just not a smart thing to do. Why would anyone put himself in a compromising position like that? Why tempt fate?" He admitted that I was right. But the truth of the matter is, I would never have known if something had happened to him, because this type of assault would probably never have made it into the media in Boston.

To people who are not brought up in the city, please do *not* judge us. We are survivors, even though as children we may have had only a pair of blue or red sneakers from Woolworth's Five and Dime, a few toys, and shared tiny closets in our small apartments, however it forced us to either sink or swim. It forced me and others to use our imaginations and to be more inventive. We in the city were rich in other ways. I lived close to work and had a lot less responsibilities with a lot more freedom. We had fun with many friends of all nationalities, ages and sizes, some whom we could trust with our lives. There was always someone around if a ride was needed, or you just wanted company to go shopping, to the doctor, or visit a neighbor for an afternoon of talk over a cup of coffee, or whatever. We also learned who not to turn our backs on which was a great lesson, sometimes learned the hard way. Yet, when we were a little older, the games got rougher and sometimes people got hurt. When that happened, it was the topic of discussion for weeks, almost like a sports event. We'd ask, "What happened? How are they? Who won and who did it?" It's hard to explain to you, but it was a way of life that made me a better, more aware person, with stronger instincts for self-survival. Unfortunately, not having lived in the city for awhile, I'm sometimes less aware than I was in those days.

As a child, in our second apartment, on Claybourne Street, my mother would say, "You're watching too much television, get out of this house and get some fresh air for a change!!" Then, I'd call my special little friends next door and if they weren't home, I'd call the girl across the street on the first floor and/or up the street. We would sit on the front steps of our multi-family buildings, in the fresh air, staring at the clouds, talking or playing cards. One night we were all out in the street looking for the Big Dipper, and catching fireflies in our small but comfortable yards, where I planted a few peach pits, and my dead turtle (at least I pray he was already dead). Every time I smell the clean night air of summer my heart is back on Claybourne Street. I haven't seen a firefly in about thirty years. Did we catch too many? I wish someone older had told us to admire them from afar. I guess the Native Americans tried to teach us. It made as much sense as catching grasshoppers and putting them in jars. I recently told a child, "You have to put him back because his mother will miss him." She immediately understood, and she quickly set him FREE.

I finally decided to move from the city when I was in my mid twenties, after a disturbing incident, which was the straw that broke the camel's back for me. An elderly Irish woman on our block was punched in the face a few times and robbed of her pocketbook by a black man, who had followed her home from the bank. Pretending to be lost he asked for directions.

A lot of my childhood friends from the city own their own businesses, others have good jobs, a few are housewives who haven't HAD to work. Many now live in the suburbs, a few have been in jail, and some have passed away. Many have kicked their addiction to drugs and/or alcohol. Don't feel sorry for city kids. Pray to clean up yourself, your OWN homes, and your neighborhoods. In 1999, forty percent of the drug problems are in the city, sixty percent are in the suburbs. Don't offer me pity, just offer me love and/or a job. To people who feel they're being held back, don't use lame excuses for not being able to go forward, or seek out ways to blame OTHERS for holding you back, when it is your own negative laziness which is the real cause of your failure. It's called, I feel sorry for me, who do you feel sorry for? I know because "I've been there, done that." I went through a phase of my own laziness and confusion of just cruising through life. For some of my life I was a grasshopper and now I'm an ant. Do you enter the race of life *to win* or just *hang in* 'till it's over? Learn what you're here for and accomplish it! Attention all snobs... remember it takes ALL kinds to make this world go around! Let's save our helping hands for the poor souls from the war, the people that are unfairly being pushed out of mental hospitals onto society's cold, un-welcoming streets, as well as homeless kids and cats. Please help children whose guardians make them live with abuse, alcoholism, filth and squalor. In Boston alone *twenty* children a night need a bed to sleep in. Do you have an extra room? Call foster care NOW!! I love myself now because of how hard I have worked on myself, not because I have more toys. So please don't judge me. Judge yourself! Be happy, centered, loving and everything else will come together for you and your family.

Help me to do so God. *Okay!*

As I mentioned before, when I met Christina I was living in a big *eerie* house on Adams Street, which was over one hundred-twenty years old. The house had been one of the original homes in a nice neighborhood of mostly single family homes. It sat on a beautiful quarter acre of land across from Cedar Grove Cemetery and in front of Dorchester Park. It was just up the street from Saint Gregory's Church, and Baker's Chocolate Factory on the Dorchester/Milton Lower Mills line.

Before moving into this house, my father took my mother and me for a ride to view it. While driving down the street, my father proudly asked me, "Which house do you think I bought?" I looked around at all the nice homes respectably spaced on the main street and said, "I don't care, as long as it's not THAT house." Even though I did care because they bought the house without me. I didn't mean to hurt his feelings, but that WAS the house he purchased. At the time, I had no idea why I said that. After living there a short while, it became very clear to me that it was haunted by more than one ghost. No wonder I don't like surprises! I believe one of the spirits helped me get a scholarship to the Museum of Fine Arts in Boston, because prior to living there I didn't have artistic desires at all.

While some were competing with the Jones's, city people were competing about who was the poorest. One person would say, "We had eight people sleeping in a bed."

The next would ask, "Oh, you had a bed?"

A guy I had a crush on when I was younger hurt my feelings one day, by telling me that he was jealous of me. When I asked him why, his reply was, "Because you had a yard. I lived on the top floor in a triple-decker, on only a very small piece of property."

I said, "So did I, when I was younger."

Then someone else piped up and said, "Where I lived we had no yard at all, just cement." He won!! It never phased me either way whether someone had more or less than I.

I felt sad leaving my grade school friends on the other side of town, but it meant meeting Christina and other new good friends, such as a good looking guy named Thomas Finneran who asked me out just before he got into politics, and before he met and married another girl named Donna. Now he is the Speaker of the House. You just never know. Anyway, they all changed my life forever. That's a gift we receive from everyone we meet. Be kind!

It wasn't until my late teens that I realized Christina held a lot of anger and sadness inside to appease and make *others* happy and to keep and make peace for everybody, out of fear of arguments. For that reason, everyone loved her. You're too good to be true! Christina died in 1990 of cancer, leaving behind a very young daughter and two young sons. Even as I write this, I feel that numb feeling or no feeling, dreamlike state coming over me, like not REALLY being here. Or maybe it's not wanting to be here on a subconscious level, dredging up old, sorrowful feelings of loss.

***

February 1999: I saw the movie, "Terms of Endearment," with Shirley MacClaine and Jack Nicholson on TV. I cried because her daughter in the movie died of cancer leaving behind a very young daughter and two young sons. After re-reading the previous paragraph, I'm not as sad as when I originally wrote it in 1997, so it does get easier. An old saying goes, "Life by the yard is hard, life by the inch is a cinch."

I attended one of Shirley's spiritual weekend seminars in Boston, over ten years ago. I was looking around the room at approximately a thousand people from all walks of life, when I felt a pulling at me to turn around, as I did I was looking right into Shirley MacClaine's eyes. After making eye contact with me, she shivered with spiritual recognition and then, after a couple of tries finally pulled her gaze away. Shirley, thank you so much for going "Out on a Limb" sharing all of your wonderful knowledge with so many people.

Shirley's books are easy, informative reading.

***

Cancer is a grievous deep secret of hate. It's a deep hidden hurt, a resentment that's been around for a long, long time. It eats away at your mind, body and soul... until you die. It's a feeling of "WHY BOTHER, WHAT'S THE USE?" Say the following affirmation many times so that your mind will program your body, and help put you on the healing road:

> *I approve of myself and everything that I do in love, and with love, for myself NOW. I choose to forgive myself and let go of all the past, in a loving way. I now completely fill my universe with happiness, calmness and love.*

My mother said this affirmation is like a love-letter to yourself.

Maybe, if Christina had spoken her mind, she'd be alive today. Maybe if she drank healthier, decaffeinated teas, and at least eight glasses of water at room temperature a day, ate the right foods and avoided meat, fish, etc., she'd still be here. I gave up meat, especially veal, due to the fact that it's very unhealthy for you, because of the inhumane way they're raised. I lost twelve pounds within two weeks, and my cholesterol is perfect. I've never eaten lobster, and I've since given up fish and I feel better - lighter! About a year before Christina passed away, she told me she could never eat cabbage because it would always make her deathly ill. So I asked my holistic nutritionist why that was. He told me, "Cabbage is a natural way to fight cancer, as is broccoli and certain other vegetables and foods. When you start to detoxify with healthier foods and liquids, sometimes you tend to get ill before you get well. The toxins start to move around and eventually escape from your body causing headaches, fungus nails, tiredness and even flu and allergy-like symptoms, among other things. At least two ways I know of having fungus nails, athletes foot, ETC., are; you have an overabundance of fungus/yeast in your body, as a result of that it's being pushed out, or if you didn't have the symptoms till you started an inner cleansing program - your body is now FORCING the fungus out of you."

It's no wonder Christina and other people are sick and unhealthy in general due to the fact that our schools basically feed us junk food. Also most hospital food is not good for healthy people let alone sick people and children. The governmental systems are not finished with us yet, you'd think they have a big insurance policy out on us because nursing homes usually just leave unhealthy food in front of dysfunctional people. "Meals on wheels" feed elderly people things I wouldn't even feed my stray cats, such as food they can't even chew let alone digest, like corn or hot dogs and beans. I can't even eat those NOW! Use *common sense*, please give them healthy pureed food without them *having* to ask for it.

When I would tell Christina and others they needed to go to a "HOLISTIC nutritionist" they would cheerfully say, maybe later or "I've been to a nutritionist in the hospital."

My holistic nutritionist asked about my job, home life and childhood. It was then I realized by my mom's symptoms at age eighty, that she had yeast problems when I was born passing it into my cells and creating in me illness, weepy or crying jags, sadness, and as a child, wanting to be left alone. This occurred especially after I ate yeast related food, tonics (soda), and even store bought juices. At the time none of us knew why I acted that way. The Candida yeast problems resulted as I grew older, in my craving for "an alcoholic drink" such as beer, wine, etc. I also craved ice cream, candy, raisins, peanut butter, chocolate, sugar, flour and vinegar products, etc., which *feeds* yeast, as plant food feeds plants. My nutritionist told me to eat breads without yeast, flour, sugar, etc. in them, (Health food stores have these products, although some of the bigger markets are starting to wake up), or in a pinch use Pita bread. I was also told to buy Artichoke Spaghetti which I love, kidney beans, Soy or Rice drink and a greener lettuce because it's healthier for you, iceberg lettuce is hard to digest, as meat is. There's a lot to learn about what our grandmothers already knew, such as don't forget to factor in a *positive attitude*. When I changed my diet to "yeast free" and gave up the addictive coffee, my allergies and runny nose, among other symptoms went away. I also lost weight and inches which I couldn't do before, because it was more yeast than FAT in me.. meaning no matter how little I ate I couldn't lose weight. I still have a puffy stomach and thighs, one reason is from the accident which seven hospitals and three clinics didn't help me with. All they did was give me more drugs, I didn't even fill half of the prescriptions because I knew they were making me worse, but the doctors wouldn't believe me. As a matter of fact, one doctor said I would not accept the fact that I was OBESE. I'd never been fat in my whole life! Although I *thought* I was in my teens and twenties, when I was only five to ten pounds over weight. My old pictures prove I was skinny. I have a big box filled with more stories about this situation. The owner of a company I worked for *made* me carry ten steel flags which were a lot taller than me, and when I went to put some of them down I got a sharp pain in my lower back and then across my stomach. The minute that happened my stomach started to get puffy, eventually after a couple of years, I looked seven months pregnant and still growing. It *might* also be that I flipped my bowel creating seepage into my whole system, and constipation. If it wasn't for herbs and all the alternative things I mention in this book I would be dead now. A person where I live said to me, "You have what I have - a HERNIA!" I replied, my M.R.I. didn't show one. I STILL have to keep up with my problem but it's not nearly as bad as it was. When you hurt yourself mentally and/or physically it creates or allows yeast to come in and makes matters worse than they already are. Eating yeast related foods was not helping me. Now I'm going seven days a week and can't find healthy, vegetarian, inexpensive, fast foods. Just because I'm out a lot, and I'm doing certain exercises, doesn't mean I'm exercising my thighs enough. Most of the time all I do is get in and out of the car! Also connecting tissue and fat retain fluids creating a condition called cellulite around our stomach, hips, thighs and buttocks. That must be where my chocolate and eight glasses of water are going! I recently took cellulite pills and some of the puffiness went away. Our bodies *need* a certain amount of fat, through *vegetable fats,* such as Olive Oil. The change of food and eating habits is hard at first, one reason being I had to eat good food six times a day. Once you start eating better and then feeling better, there's nothing like it. Since people are different and have their OWN agenda of living experiences, everyone needs their own holistic prescription for health. Although you'd be surprised the groups of people I meet who have similar stories, with the same screens of denial over their/our eyes, although sometimes I just didn't know any better. I also heal people by going into their homes, and/or offices to see what might be affecting them negatively there, so we can cleanse it and them. Three doctors have proven that you can't use your family genes as an excuse any longer because it makes up only thirty-five percent of your health expectancies. They said, if you take good care of yourself it would override your gene pool. Otherwise why would only one sibling, out of say seven siblings, get the disease or have a heart attack or have lung problems, etc.? I'm not buying that they're the only one who contracted or inherited "the virus-germ-gene, or anything else!" Most of us CREATE it. It's a tough pill to swallow, and admit that you're not perfect and you HAVE TO CHANGE to learn your lessons and survive. I know this because even though, for a big part of my life, I thought I was the exact opposite of perfect, I still didn't want to face what I needed to face, which was the reality of knowing on some level that I had to do better, which translated into "there is something WRONG with ME." Then I learned you can't accomplish what you came here for without change -- equaling growth!! I feel that I must have taken a VOW of poverty and pain from heaven, because I've been sick a lot since birth, and whenever I became financially established it's taken from me again and again. So I feel I was obviously born into sickness, predestined if you will, but it took me all these years of searching and correcting it, to be out of pain and suffering. Unfortunately a lot of healers have to suffer, and learn how not to suffer anymore, in order to help others heal. This is one of the many reasons for me to share this book with you, to show you in a simple way a lot of what I've learned with God's help. This is what we're looking at in this book. Do we create our own problems, are we born into our family's stuff or are we just predestined? Which are you? There's ALWAYS someone who is now saying, "Why didn't you meditate or visualize, or *whatever* your needs and therefore create them?" I've done it all a million times, when it is MY time...it will happen! I ALSO believe that part of the problem is, the more powerful you are and you think one tiny little negative thing, THAT'S what you bring to yourself. My dear friends and I have been visualizing this book forever, it just wasn't time before now! Visualizing is getting a mental picture of what you want and then picturing it happening again, and again. Do *not* visualize anything negative, or try to take another person's mate, or you *will* pay tenfold. To the people who are questioning every little thing, please STOP THINKING, and just take through your soul what YOU need from this book! Getting back to genes, I asked a scientist who specializes in that field, why dogs look like their masters? They're working on it! It's probably past life stuff.

When I moved into where I live now, in November of 1994, I quickly discovered that also living in this building was a poltergeist named Dennis, among a lot of other ghosts. No they didn't follow me here, they might have brought me here to help them go to the *other side*. I was SUPPOSED to move somewhere else, I even had a certified check for another apartment in my pocketbook. It will all be in my book named "Dennis," which I feel will be made into a movie. Babe Ruth came here in spirit in "1996" and visited for a long time. Other V.I.S., "Very Important Spirits" came by, such as Princess Di, Frank Sinatra, Lucille Ball, and Linda McCartney, as well as others. They all had messages and were very interesting to be with. Babe is *very* strong in spirit as he was in body on this earth, but that's another book - I will get to it after this one, God willing! Anyway, I drink Vodka once in a while, but all of a sudden I found I could not pass a package store. Dennis was *making* me CRAVE in the worst way of all things...GIN. He even made me buy green Creme-de-Menthe and other liquors, such as beer (which I would NEVER buy because of the yeast), with the little money I had left over from moving. He was like a kid in a candy store, only with MY money and MY liver! By the second bottle of Gin within about a month, a lot of broken things in my apartment, the TV going off and on, loud banging noises in the attic and much, *much* more, I was desperately calling around seeking help. A spiritual group said they would come by a couple of times, but when they had to cancel for whatever reason, Dennis became enraged and broke even more things. One time he broke my mother's favorite depression glass, which *was* in a *closed* cabinet. It took me awhile but a Spiritual Church was kind enough to finally rescue me as well as the big pest, I mean the spirit who showed me new lessons, the IRISH man named

Dennis. Apparently, Dennis had created a lot of anger because he was tired of being stuck on this earth and wanted to leave, he sensed I could help him. Some nice people who didn't even know me, from a Spiritual church, drove almost an hour to my home and we all helped send Dennis into the light. It was still sad to me, like being at a funeral, then Dennis said, "Donna, I'm Sorry!" After asking forgiveness he quickly disappeared. This proves to me just about ANYONE can get into heaven!!

After Dennis left, no more of my things were broken and the incessant banging in the attic stopped, but other incidences went on. To make a long story short, this book is NOT intended to diagnose you or anyone else. I can only give you my life stories on what helped create my heavy drinking, mostly in my early twenties. Getting a lot of messages you don't understand from spirits, as well as seeing things, hearing things, smelling things such as flowers and pets who have passed away, that other people might not be tuned into, can be very confusing and scary without a psychic mentor to help show you the way. Drinking, drugs, shopping, gambling, etc. helps numb the reality of spiritualism. That's why, I feel, there are so many spiritual people in support groups such as Alcoholics Anonymous.

Back to yeast: Yeast was probably my father's problem also, as he drank and smoked in the years before I was born. He had bouts of depression at various times in his life, which is also a symptom of too much yeast. Christina probably had yeast problems as well. Other symptoms to look for are earaches, asthma, fatigue, headaches, anxiety, acne, skin-irritations, constipation, diarrhea, allergies, muscle weakness, persistent coughs, recurrent vaginitis and more. If you or someone you know have some of these symptoms, I strongly suggest you buy a book on Candida and yeast infections. You may find a way to alleviate the problem. It's not written in stone that you have a yeast problem but it IS AN ALTERNATIVE if your doctor can't cure you. When I typed "muscle weakness," I thought of the accident again - when I pulled muscles in my stomach and back, which led to more serious problems. This book is helping to heal me. If you take a lot of antibiotics it can create serious yeast infections also. As I mentioned before, I've changed my diet and I no longer crave alcohol, flour and sugar products, although it took years for the results to occur, because it took awhile for the yeast and it's repercussions to occur. I want to put a disclaimer here in case you ever see me eating chocolate, I feed my soul chocolate, *once in a while*, to keep it happy, and quiet! I gave up everything else!! I KNOW it's not good for the yeast, I never said I was perfect but I'm trying! Everything in moderation.

We are also sometimes born into our relatives' sins and even parasites which create some incurable diseases. We also catch worms from our partners and even from dirty hands. Parasites "do not always" show up in human or animal stool samples, even though you might have them. Tapeworms *never* show up in stool samples. Worms *never* show up in X-rays and can help create yeast and toxin problems. All the jogging, vitamins and antibiotics in the world will *only* make the worms healthier, although it's better than lying down and doing nothing. Per a doctor's report, parasites thrive on "stressed" cells. You, your family and your pets need to take a herbal *mixture* parasite cleanser quite often for the first year to kill off the resilient egg, larvae and parasite. After a year if you feel TOTALLY sure you are free of *everything* (Do the herbs kill *everything*?) you can cut back to about twice a year to prevent new infestations from our food, water and restaurants. Don't forget about the rich pet food companies who get away with putting disgusting, contaminated, unknown meats in their food products. They sometimes contain road kill, parasites and dog collars were even found within the past couple of years. W*ash your hands and clean under your nails! I'm not saying every one has parasites. I just want to empower YOU so that you can prevent yourself, your family and your pets from contracting them. You will have energy that you have not experienced in many years! One* doctor *states,* you will find yourself healing from sicknesses which traditional medicine is not able to address. Such as excess weight, back pain, anemia, allergies, teeth grinding and *much* more. *It would be easy for* *you to go into denial right now saying that you don't have parasites, but that same doctor says about 90% of us do.*

Insist on cleaner restaurants and healthier pet foods.

Doctors and scientists - I have a challenge for you. A lot of people I've taken care of, and also people I've seen on TV, have two similar marks, one sometimes a little larger than the other, *usually* at close proximity to each other which can start out as scabs, then turn brown, looking sometimes like two freckles. Sometimes they're just flesh colored bumps, *not* similar to pimples. Some weeks they inadvertently appear, other weeks they may not come out at all. These people usually end up in wheel chairs or bed-ridden, crippled physically, mentally and spiritually. I feel that these marks are caused by parasites found ONLY in humans. These are NOT to be confused with a large amount of natural freckles or broken blood vessels and may appear anywhere on the body. The jury is still out on age marks though. Some can be cancerous. Yet why do some people have them and some don't?

In "1999": In my unscientific research of parasites in the last couple of years, I've asked quite a few doctors what they thought of the problem. Two doctors asked if a lot of Chinese food was eaten because they don't know what's in it, in some of the restaurants. Two Dermatologists said the two marks look safe and would not biopsy them. One Doctor who specializes in parasites, and costs $200.00 dollars *an hour, and is very busy*, said there's no parasite which can go through the skin, they might be from fleas. Check with your vet and regular doctor. That doesn't make sense to me. A vet was consulted and he had never seen them before. I also mentioned having clothes with *two holes* in them which matched up with the two marks on the body. The doctor just looked confused. A few doctors changed the subject by saying in a very condescending way, or laughingly, it's not parasites unless the person eats a lot of Sushi or has visited a third world country, therefore it must be ANOTHER illness. (What about someone from a third world country serving you food, or dating someone who's visited another country, or contracted parasites as a child from eating dirt or sucking on rocks, which is a craving due to a vitamin and mineral deficiency.) Some doctors agree that the majority of people have parasites. Didn't they all learn the same things in medical schools??

I asked a nurse in a clinic what she thought about parasites. The conversation turned to seeing a worm in fish at a restaurant, in which we had both frequented.

She freaked out and said, "They can't stay in your system."

I replied, "Look in any home medical book. It will tell you differently."

It turns out I know five people, including us, who have seen worms in fish at that same busy restaurant. I also met a man recently who owns a fish store, who does *not* eat fish for that very reason. Hot dogs, meat and pork are also on *the list*.

My first powerful mentor, who was WAY ahead of his time, was a psychic, holistic healing doctor and acupuncturist. When I met him over twenty-five years ago, I felt almost an instant connection with him. The first time I ever heard the word "healer" was from him. My first intentional healing lessons began because I had been sick on and off most of my life. In my twenties, I took myself to many doctors who gave me yet more pills and almost right after taking them, I got migraines, colitis and allergies, all incurable. All of a sudden, I was allergic to cats even though I had them all my life with no problems, and fourteen other things including dust! Migraines, the doctors had no cure for back then, they said it was *psychological*. For colitis, they give an operation called a colostomy, it's a bag attached to your body from your colon. I had gone to many hospitals and doctors for a couple of years, to no avail. Finally, thank God, someone told me about acupuncture, which back then was almost illegal here. Apparently doctors didn't want to lose business so they said it wasn't safe, and if cured it was *psychological*, even though it's been used elsewhere for thousands of years. This is how naive I could be, I use to think all doctors had a calling to heal people. My doctor, mentor, life saver, named Dr. Moore, cured me within about a week through acupuncture, he also advised such things as, diet, yoga, vitamins, and that even if you're sick take a shower or a bath. Doctor Moore also showed me that I was worthy of good things in life, and as a result I had a new found respect for my soul, mind, body and life. I realized my body was on overload and could hold no more chemicals ("99"My lessons on yeast in the blood was years later. I had an overload of yeast to begin with. Those pills, very probably, pushed it over the edge). I still fight off everyday problems which our bodies usually do in a NATURAL way. As I mentioned before, my smoking, drinking, the stress and confusion of ghosts and psychic messages wearing my brain down, didn't help either. Doctor Moore, my *teaching* doctor, started telling me about parasites back then. I freaked out saying, "I don't want to know about that!"

(Thank you God, for not letting me lose these new finishing touches throughout this chapter, May 26, 1999, Wednesday!!! I borrowed an old computer from Shirley this month and only learned the basics, then "somehow" the nine hours of work went into "Never-Never Land" with Tinker Bell on May 9, 1999. I was *not* happy. When I went to Sam and Jan's new computer the work was GONE!)

He sternly said to me, "But you NEED to know."

(My father used to say similar things to me.)

I asked, "Why?" Dr. Moore didn't answer me. But now it's obvious isn't it? Doctor, thank you so much for all you taught and showed me, it means a lot to me and others whom I have since helped with your shared knowledge. Since he moved out of state, I went to other acupuncturists who were not as good, so please be careful.

When I feel I'm losing myself I think of Dr. Moore and he comes to my side as in astral projection, meaning he's come out of his physical body but is still alive and visits me. Or his thoughts come to me through mental telepathy, to help me regain my strength, making me feel as if I'm not alone. Elderly people do that all the time. Healers also do these thing a lot, mostly during the night, to help heal people all over the world. I've had people tell me that I came to them in a dream and helped them, I don't remember it at all. There dreams came true! I also go back, in my mind, and relax into the comfort of my doctor's sensitive lessons. Once you learn all you can from one teacher you must move onto the next teacher, even if you don't want to leave the first one, it's MEANT to BE.

Someone told me their child got worms from a sand box, per her doctor. I believe it because on TV they said the beach isn't good for your pets due to so many fleas in the sand.

Another doctor, from a clinic whom I questioned, mentioned that he gives patients with parasites, who come from third world countries, a prescription of three little yellow pills, which cost more than fifty dollars. The color of these pills look suspiciously like *the same* color liquid medication the vet gave to my cats, which is for round worms, pin worms, and hook worms, it's called Strongid T (for a LOT less money). Droncit, a white pill which cost me two dollars a pill, is for tapeworms. I make sure my cats, even the strays, get one dose of both medications within a week to ten days of the first dose, once a year. PETA suggested if given too frequently they could cause *neurological* problems and Strongid T can cause *respiratory* problems as well. When I have the money I give my cats a parasite herbal mixture (which is very expensive), rather than the vets medicine. My cats' stool samples *never* showed parasites, as a matter of fact, the day after a negative stool sample one cat had a tapeworm on her anus and a day later the other cat had a round worm on hers. As I said before, tapeworms *never* show up in stool samples, so most vets *never* treat them! The first cat had constipation among other symptoms, and the second cat had diarrhea and vomiting. Kidney disease is a potential danger later in life if too much of the afore- mentioned drugs are given. Too many doses of these drugs can cause resistance in the parasites. Check with your vet on how far apart to give these drugs (don't give too much), but don't allow him to talk you out of it! I found unfortunately, like OUR doctors, they all have different answers. Maybe they were absent from medical school that day? Scary!! I had a receptionist give me the wrong advice, be careful. When looking at the original container of Strongid-T at the vet's, I noticed the label said it is safe for HUMAN *consumption*. However, I *wouldn't* advise you to try it on your own because it's prescribed by your weight. The only worms that could be life threatening to your cats, per PETA, are hookworms and heartworms. Heartguard makes a pill that if given on a monthly schedule, prevents both these parasites from surviving in your cat's body. Check with your vet to see about a prescription. Someone had a homeless cat put to sleep because it was *infested* with tapeworms.

I asked the doctor at the clinic who gave the pills, "What about a SECOND prescription for your patients, due to the fact that eggs and larvae don't come out for about a week or so later, depending on the moon?"

He replied, "No. I don't give that." Then he blurted out, almost surprising himself, "You should see what I had to do to get rid of MY parasites!" An angel must have made him say it. NO, he hadn't visited another country.

I quickly asked him, "What did you have to do?" He ran from the room and never returned any of my many calls. It was as if he had let out a big secret.

I asked an internist, at a hospital in town, if he had ever seen those two spots on a persons body.

He said: "Yes, many times."

I asked: "What are they?"

He responded: "I don't know."

I asked: "Did you ever biopsy them?"

He said: "No."

I asked: "Why?"

He answered: "Because they look innocent enough."

I looked at him and mirrored softly what he had said...."They *look* INNOCENT enough." We have a right to an accurate, informative answer given to us with respect, in layman's terms, for EVERY mark on our bodies.

I even called an 800 number which was on the back of an "enzyme package," and told the previous story to a doctor who had answered the phone. The doctor laughed, then told me a story about how when he was a kid in the 1950's living in New York, his doctor checked him every year for parasites. He went on to say that in the farming areas of Texas, the doctors automatically de-wormed children EVERY year. Then in the

"60's," it became UNFASHIONABLE to speak of parasites and treatment of them unfortunately stopped.

I then said, "So our children are in big trouble."

He answered, "YES. I believe a lot of childhood diseases are caused by parasites. Kids crave and eat a lot of sugar, which feeds parasites."

I answered, "I also believe this and have heard about it someplace before. I hope we find our way back to the old ways."

He said, "So do I."

Isn't it ironic that in the '60's we also started killing ourselves with pesticides and chemicals?

Doctor Hulda Clark has a ground-breaking book called 'The Cure for All cancers' claims that most cancers are caused by a parasite and that every single one of her patients with cancer *had parasites*. Once Doctor Clark eliminated their parasites, the tumors also *disappeared. I wish I knew this in time to help Christina.*

They recently found a man who had been frozen for more than *two thousand* years. Scientists discovered parasites in his system, although that wasn't the cause of death. Why is it *so* difficult for doctors to find them in humans *today*, when they know parasites exist in us? In California they use a blood test to find parasites. I feel that everyone should see a sample of their own blood under a microscope. Seeing any of your illnesses through sick red, and white blood cells, too much sugar, etc., up close like that "would change your life." A health food store could direct you to a qualified person who tests blood, and in doing that they can also tell you what herbs and minerals you're lacking.

I just met a lovely eighty-three year old woman who is suffering a lot of pain. During my holistic research I was questioning her about the numerous sets of spots and bites on her back, varying in size from very small, flat, innocent looking pairs to the huge, ugly, thumb-sized pair of dark brown welts. She told me her story of how she liked to dance to jazz when she was a young woman. However, in her early twenties she started getting shaking movements in her legs with a little pain, now progressively worsening. Most of the time she still cannot get comfortable because she feels a crawling movement within her legs, which changes to excruciating pain and then the shaking starts. She also *sometimes* feels a tingling or a small pinch yet *sees nothing* before the two marks appear. The pain in her back is so severe that she can't lay flat in her bed. She must sit up all night and can't sleep because of the pain. She said it's a horrible feeling all over her body and the pain and shaking is also in her arms. For all intents and purposes this woman has suffered most of her life.. over sixty years. She is almost out of money, and she said the government won't pay for her medical bills, *because she doesn't lie down at night.* The logic being, she's well enough to sit up!!! The doctors are still working on a diagnosis, but they say anyone can get it at any age.

There's a foundation called "The Restless Legs Syndrome," At, RLS Foundation, PO Box 7050, Dept. DH, Rochester, Minnesota 55903-7050. Someone described their symptoms as a creepy-crawly, pulling sensation deep in their legs. They went on to say, they have to walk around or pound on their legs to make these feelings go away. Though the exact cause of this baffling disorder remains *elusive*, work is in progress to find the answers. If you would like to know more about RLS, please send a self-addressed, 55cent stamped, #10 business sized envelope to the prior address.

I'm not a rocket scientist, but it seems to me if you put the movement together with these spots, you'll see they're giving people a prolonged sickness and sending them to an early grave. Doctors or scientists, prove me RIGHT or WRONG! Please don't use the BIG WORD meaning, *"I DON'T KNOW!"* I suggest you find the answer before you or yours feels the incurable, crippling pain for the rest of your lives, or see the small to hideous looking, dangerous marks appearing on your bodies. Do biopsies and test on PEOPLE for accuracy. Some medicines tested on animals cause an adverse reaction and even death in humans. If it's a pill for humans, test on humans! There are more *accurate* ways to test today, without using animals, per humane foundations. However, they have to PAY people. It's cheaper paying people to steal our pets off our streets, and from ads in the newspapers, to use in experimental labs. Sometimes the government takes their quota from animal rescue leagues for the training of the military. They release these animals, then recapture them; then they bludgeon, strangle or decapitate these poor animals. Please write to Secretary of defense William Cohen, Washington, D.C. to stop this cruelty. Make them pick on someone their own size. Please donate to researchers who *DO NOT* test on animals.

I saw an old Vincent Price movie named "The Tingler". It was about strange looking things that live in our bodies and they have two large stingers on their heads and two smaller ones on their tails. At the end of the show Vincent told the audience, *beware* EVERYONE has them and they live on fear.

In 1999 I met this beautiful little girl who on her arm had two tiny round scabs and on her leg had two dark brown spots which look like freckles. What am I suppose to tell her, not only do doctors not have a cure, they don't even know what I'm talking about.

***

Back to Christina's cancer: Did Christina preprogram herself for cancer, because her father had died at a young age of cancer? Did she take after him by stuffing things and negative emotions into her body and cells, instead of confessing her true feelings? That, as a result, released deadly poisons which were bottled up in her, creating sick blood cells. Christina also missed her mother, who had suffered and died of cancer two years before Christina's death. Maybe they all had an agreement before they were born into this life, to be together, to get cancer and die early, and to learn lessons from each other on what to do to prevent illness. Destinies can be changed. The question is should they all be changed? Get into your *zone* and stay *focused*! Only the strong survive. As my mother always said, "It's a great life, if you don't weaken."

A holistic (mind, body, soul) doctor would have looked into all of these health factors. I was awake to spiritualism and healing, but Christina would not listen to me or anyone else but "the doctors." She had given up smoking about a year before she passed away. I had given up smoking more than two packs of Camels a day fifteen years before, because I was finding it hard to breathe. I started when I was about twelve years old.

Written on 1/29/99 8 P.M.

About sixteen years ago, I had three non-malignant lumps removed from my left breast at different times. One female doctor not only removed the wrong lump, but she also "forgot" to write it in my files. So when I asked the nurses to check my operation they just argued with me and stormed out of the room. I was made to go back by yet another doctor to have the correct lump removed, which was NOT lot of "fun" because I WAKE UP during operations, and I dislike hospitals.

If the first doctor had *taught* me how to nurture myself so I would not have created another fibroid cyst, or possibly brought it a step further to cancer, I would not have needed the second and third operations. I was in a bad relationship for years, and I knew that was a big part of the problem. No-one said life was going to be easy! Back then, I promised God if I got another lump, it would stay with me 'till I died a natural death, or it would kill me. Predestined?

Shortly after, the fourth lump was in the right breast this time. After the mammogram was taken, I went to a healing circle. A very POWERFUL healer, to whom I had a very strong connection, was there. The next day I went for my final X-rays. The doctor was arguing with me, trying to get me to have *another* operation. However, as he held up the X-ray, he couldn't find the lump.

He became outraged and bellowed, "Where did it go?"

I replied, "I don't know." He held up the previous X-ray from two weeks before. The lump was plainly visible on the first X-ray.

He kept *yelling* at me, "What happened to it?"

I admitted to the nurse after he left, that I had been to a healer, because she had kept asking me, "What happened to the lump?" She was very interested in my explanation. I have since realized that many nurses have left their professions to start their own holistic businesses and journeys. My promise to God is not to be confused with the people who let their children die, by not getting them medical treatment in the name of their religion. So I say over and over again, "Go to the doctors first, then baffle them by healing yourself using holistic complementary medicine, alternative methods, holistic hypnotists, holistic nutritionists, healers, powerful magnets, crystals, TAI CHI, etc. Think positive happy thoughts, smile and then trust God and yourself. Create your good health and positive dreams!"

I've healed myself quickly of sore throats and cold sores, and haven't had a cold or flu in many years. I become symptomatic when I'm detoxifying from everyday pollutions, such as our processed foods, pesticides, antibiotics, contaminants from food, water and the air we breathe. You must get rid of the build-up of toxins in your system, or you will not be protected against disease. All of these WILL Lead to digestive problems, blemishes, fatigue, ALLERGIES and general poor health, maybe leading (if not rectified) to more SERIOUS problems. You have to cleanse your insides a few times a year as well. Remember castor oil, Soda Mint tablets and enemas as a child? Hopefully you clean inside your mouth and ears ... the enema is the same idea. It also wouldn't kill you to fast once in a while to give your system a rest. Read up on these things so you'll find the right cleansers and fasts for you, or ask your holistic nutritionist. Don't forget to use organic foods, or all foods, and juicer drinks as if they were medicines, and remember your stomach is only as big as your fist. Gravy is grease, blood and flour. It's important for you to know that micro-waves get food hot but they don't kill bacteria. Don't grill or bake potatoes with aluminum foil on them because the potato skins do not get hot enough to eliminate botulism. Open a window once in a while and breathe deeply. Exercise with light weights, it's especially good for your bones. Do Yoga, drink plenty of water, chew your food well, dance, meditate and listen to all types of tapes, even comedy. Remember your skin is the largest organ your body has, so walk (using sun screen), and exercise till you perspire so the toxins come out through your skin more quickly, even if only for a half hour a couple of times a week. Take a relaxing bath, steam, sauna or read a book. Also try a HOLISTIC chiropractor, masseuse, etc., *or else* pick out a wheel chair now for your seventies and eighties, IF you make it that far. Take good care of yourself. You deserve it...I deserve it!!

Remember there is evidence now, that prayer really works. A group of patients who had been prayed for had less complications, than the ones who were not prayed for. One doctor who helped with that research, now prays before operating on anyone. There is now a group who uses prayer to lose weight. THE PRAYERS ARE WORKING, they ARE losing weight! What these prayers are really doing, is keeping Satan at arms length, as a result keeping the dieters out of harm's way, so he doesn't force them to desire an overabundance of food. I think all the unfortunate people who sleep walk should pray hard and often, but especially those who get up and eat raw meats, etc. I can help you with the issues that go along with that; such as: how old were you when it started? Do you remember anything that happened to you, or anything you might have done or thought to let Satan in, creating a dark side in you? If we're not careful, we may get emotionally STUCK at the young age, when a trauma happened to us. No matter how small it seems, it needs to be cleansed out of you. And when as adults, if you're very sensitive, you can hear it come up in yourself or another person, especially when provoked. Example: You're acting like a child! That's the time to find out, how old you were and what happened to you at that age?? Then let it go. The same with bulimic and anorexic people and others, PRAY to release your demons! Even if the doctors have found a physical abnormality...PRAY!! Due to all the predictions of disaster and Armageddon (fight against good and evil), Nostradamus, Edgar Cayce and the Bible mention the time is close. Whether we like it or not, we must be prepared, and also understand that WE CAN create a better world through love and stop it from happening. The battle is NOW, Satan is trying even as you read this, to conquer you. No matter who you are, even the holy ones are not safe because to Satan that would be like capturing a General during war time. You must protect yourself at ALL times, pray before you go to sleep because that's an easy time for him to slip into you. If you wake up in a bad mood, or lose your temper during the day, PRAY. Teach your children and others to also protect themselves, or we are all LOST. Have faith ...ask and you shall receive!

When I get a symptom, I ask myself, "What am I trying to avoid, or did I cheat too much on my yeast free diet and if so, WHY?" I also try to remember if something traumatic happened recently, or up to about six months prior to my illness, because that's usually how long it takes to fester in you before its negative affects start to show up IN and/or ON your body. In any event, I immediately start giving myself rest and open to a page of positive affirmations. Whatever affirmation leaps out at me, is the one I use for most of the day unless I feel another one is needed later on. I recently learned the apostles opened inadvertently to a section in their Torah (Old Testament) for their messages. I also listen to meditation, and positive thinking tapes. If you fall asleep during them that's okay too, it still sinks in. It also helped that I gave up a "toxic relationship." Within a week of breaking up with that person, I was working with people who had flu symptoms. Weakened by the breakup, I found myself getting a sore throat. When I tried to rest, as aforementioned, my head would not shut-up, and I found myself getting a headache. I got up, put on a little makeup and went out. Within ten minutes, something released and I immediately started to feel better. When I got home, the symptoms seemed to be waiting there for me. So, I sat down and wrote a letter to my ex-boyfriend, waited two days and then I mailed it. I went to my aroma therapies and homeopathic remedies which I bought at health food stores, then my symptoms went away. Aroma therapies are essential oils which were used in Egypt as precious medicines and also for cosmetic purposes. There are *many* remedies which will immediately calm you and give you soothing effects, they help me a lot. LEARN HOW to take homeopathic remedies or they *won't* be effective. Also, using a juicer is VITAL to your health. It's all just good old fashioned common sense. Do your homework!!

I was also going through a very early menopause, as my mother did, which sometimes causes non-cancerous fibroid tumors. Obviously, I didn't know before all those operations, what I know now.

I realized years ago, that I have been healing others all of my life. But, healers sometimes need other TRUE healers and prayers to help them become well. I wish I had known when I was in high school that I had the ability to be a psychic holistic healer. I also wish I'd known, at a much earlier age, that it would be my vocation. Instead of hiding these natural abilities which we are born with, we should hone these abilities from childhood in schools up through college levels and at home. It was very disconcerting for me not knowing what direction I would be taking in life for such a long period of time. As a result, I wandered from art school to modeling and finishing school, to interior decorating classes, office work, sales, some marketing research and so much more. Everyone else seemed to know where they were heading with their lives. Although all these things were good to have in my background, and one way or another helped me throughout my life, I still felt my life was going in circles.

***

What does holistic mean? To heal the whole mind, body and soul.

Mind......creates good thoughts - good health,
bad thoughts - bad health!
We ARE what we THINK!!!

Soul......the essence of who we are, the engine that runs the car. A new engine can be placed in the body of any car. If the engine leaves the car, the body of the car cannot move. The same is true of our souls (also called ghosts and spirits) in our body. If you are *truly* ready to be healed from your sickness, and seriously want to live and learn your lessons, then I can reach your soul without your thinking mind and thoughts being in the way - your attitude will change.

Body......the body will have to follow the healing procedure, providing you treat your mind, body and soul with more respect. Your body is a map of the unhappiness or happiness in your soul and mind.

Examples: Broken heart - heart attack. Sick lungs - inability to breathe in (take in) life. You MAY say your lung problems are from smoking .. why did you light up to begin with? Was it nerves, trying to be like your friends, trying to buy time, trying to avoid something, fear of facing someone??? Perhaps some of us feel we aren't *good enough*, have a death wish and therefore abuse ourselves. Over time you create emphysema, or another disease, knowing deep down inside that someone will wait on you and nurture you.

Healer......to heal others: to assist people to help themselves become free from disease or bodily infirmity, to help make sound or whole.

***

I have another old friend who is lonely, unhappy and not feeling well. We went out to dinner, and I couldn't believe the things she was eating and drinking - and don't forget smoking. But I didn't say too much, because I have tried so many times before to help her. NO, not judge her! Yes, it's like walking down that Dorchester street unprotected. Her own choice!

Later that evening my friend said to me, "What's wrong with my stomach, it really hurts?" After so many years of abuse, other complications have set in. My old friend went on to say, "You're a healer..... HEAL me!!"

I was surprised at that comment. I have never really discussed healing with her because I know she isn't open to it. Out of concern for her obvious severe health problems, I asked her before she ate if she would like a mineral or herb to protect the lining of her stomach in a natural way. She refused, saying that she had her OWN vitamins.

I asked her, "Are they the right ones for you, because *some* are NOT to be taken with *others*. How do you know if those are the vitamins you need?"

She said, "Yes, they're okay!"

I hear this all of the time, so I attempted, one last time, to show her what she was doing to her body. I believe she thought I would put my hands on her and make it all better, so that she could go on eating, drinking and smoking the way we have been conditioned to all of our lives. She's NEVER going to stop her bad habits, and I'm not going to be able to help her heal herself. I'm so afraid of losing another good friend, I don't EVER want to live through that heart wrenching pain again. I want to feel I did all I could for her while she's still here, seeing her suffer is sad. She would, once again, not listen to me even though she called me many times with new aches, pains and problems. I called her the next day and told her to come to my house for a healing ... after she saw her doctor.

Her pride said, "Yeah, I'll see you later."

I thought, "Not if I see you first." It's a fact that closed, old ignorant ways, stubbornness, ego, laziness, and denial kills people. I've done all that I can. Now her life is in her hands and her doctor's hands. Some people just won't listen and change. They would rather be *operated* on, than change their diet or lifestyles.

I know a woman in her seventies, named Ruth, who keeps asking me over and over again, "Is everything all right?" and "What's going to happen tomorrow?" What surprises me is that when we go out in public she acts normal, you wouldn't know she's the same woman. Ruth suggested, it must be because she *lets her hair down* at home. She's a nice lady but hardly ever smiles and has a lot of frown lines. Her old driver's license has a forlorn looking face, one you would *not* want to meet in a dark alley. A cousin of Ruth's told me she has been like this all of her life, Ruth was ALWAYS high-strung, anxious, had anxiety, and always expected a lot from others, which leads to cold disappointments. It's no wonder she's on HEART medicine. As a result when Ruth started getting Alzheimer symptoms the family didn't notice it as anything different, telling helpers, "Oh-she's ALWAYS been like THAT, don't bother with a doctor!"

Meaning of HIGH-STRUNG; Easily upset or irritated. Meaning of ANXIOUS; Suffering the effects of apprehension, fear, or terror. Meaning of ANXIETY; a burdened or disquieted state of mind. All of these are symptoms of Alzheimer's, as well as other things, such as being freezing cold after perspiring. Patients also layer themselves with heavy coats and blankets, which Ruth did sometimes after having HOT drinks.

As a result of her NEGATIVE *attitude* I asked Ruth, "When you were younger, did anyone ever tell you to look for the positive side of life, and be happy?"

Ruth answered, "Yes, I especially recall my mother saying that to me quite often, as well as smile and the world smiles with you, cry and YOU CRY ALONE. I was very spoiled. My mother was a great cook. I never cooked and when I married, we went out to eat all the time. I had a lot of stress in my childhood because I was born left handed and everyone forced me to write right handed, they said I could be mental or evil."

On one of her good days Ruth laughingly said to me, "I know I come across as a little soft sometimes, but when I look around I feel that you and I are still more sane then a lot of these other people we've been thrown in together with."

I said, "I love that expression, 'THROWN in together!' "

She said, "I knew you would, that's why I told it to you. (It was as if she knew it needed to go into this book.) My mother would have thought you were 'the LAST word.' "

Her mother was around her a lot, she was a *to the point* type, like me. Her mother said through me to Ruth, "Do you know how smart you are?"

Ruth answered, "I don't think I am."

What fell out of my mouth next was, "You're as smart as *you think* you are!!"

Ruth looked down reflectively and said, "My dear mother, God rest her soul, use to say that to me all the time."

Ruth said, "You're the only one who makes me laugh."

"We have to make ourselves laugh, in this life," I said. Now, most of the time Ruth is a lot calmer. Because she wasn't improving altogether I asked, "Do you ever FEEL that God is helping you after you pray?"

Ruth retorted, "He sent me you, didn't he!"

I was taken aback with her quick response. When I received the call to visit her, I heard a voice in my head say, "Go." I have to make SURE who the voice is coming from, Satan or my Angels, sometimes I definitely know 100%, but this time I wasn't sure because it came through weak, plus I was *so* busy and it was a very long ride. I wanted to make sure it wasn't Satan taking me away from this book as well as other things. So I said to her relative, "I'll call you right back." I then meditated on it and got the message to GO more clearly and the word ABUSED. I called and said, "Yes," then learned she had been abused (no bath and *little* food) for THREE years by a white home health aide. Ruth had requested a white woman because the black women (who were sent to her home via cab, by the Government) intimidated her, ate all her food and slept all day long. As it turned out, the next white aide stole from her and lied about it, getting away with it.

Things *have to* change. When I arrived, I took her to the doctor because she was bleeding from the uterus, and had scabs and many sets of SPOTS all over her body. I practically begged her new female doctor to biopsy one set of *the spots*, (I wonder if *they* have anything to do with Alzheimer's), that were scattered especially around her leg area. The doctor's answer was to buy an expensive prescription cream, and if that was no help, she would give Ruth a different prescription in a *couple* of *weeks*. When I challenged her, asking if she *knew* what Ruth has, her reply was, "No." Then my question to her was, "How can you write out a prescription for medication, when you don't know what the problem is?"

Not used to being openly mistrusted, her answer was, "Well, Ruth HAS to come back here *anyway*."

Ruth loved this controversy and my obvious protection of her so much so that she became overwhelmed, and said to me with tears in her eyes, "You're saving a lot of lives. I don't know what it is, but there's *something* about you."

I asked, "Whose?"

Ruth said, "Me, for one, and many more!"

I said, "How do you know?"

Ruth answered, "I can SEE it, I just CAN!!"

Ruth was right, God *did* send me!

After knowing Ruth awhile, I saw that she was not an honest person. She would call God down to lie to my face, after sneakily looking through my purse as well as someone else's. I did take into account her age, etc.- not *all* elderly do that, but it happened once too often on her good days, this is something that didn't happen over night. (Unless a bad spirit keeps jumping into her?) Maybe that's why her family ignores her, and she gets home health aides who abuse, steal, and lie to her?? My mother said the Rosary at least three times a day and I'm SURE *never* stole anything in her life, except to give my things away...maybe that's why an aide intimidated her into giving her our silver tea set? I wouldn't wish that on her or anyone. Thou shalt *not* steal!!

I met a man with Alzheimer's once who was talking to *himself.* He said he was arguing with a deceased old friend who was laughing at him because he was loosing his memory.

On Ruth's bad days, I wouldn't stay around her for long periods of time, because the beginning of Alzheimer's is very depressing for me to feel, and watching her fade away is devastating. I go out with positive people after seeing her and I keep myself strong. You can sense her unhappiness and depression emitting from her, throughout the whole house, and her high IQ is no help to her any more. It seems to me that when Ruth drinks a lot of milk she acts more disoriented. There are a lot of new theories now on Alzheimer's. Some feel that it could be a virus, and some say we can have it in us from childhood, a gene which we are born with. Depending on your DIET, your clean OXYGEN intake, and if you EXERCISE, you're less likely to get Alzheimer's, the studies show. What if "that gene" from birth MAKES us lazy, and full of fear, etc., therefore we don't go for walks, etc., creating early Alzheimer's. What if, in this case, it wasn't A GENE at all but a created spoiled, lazy, dependent child wanting her own way *forever, and* as a result of that she stayed lazy and *became depressed and* FULL of FEAR of the real world in general. She never wanted to go out at all. After all, who's going to cook for her, be there to protect and stick up for her, when mother, father *and* husband are gone? All who, by the way, did NOT die of Alzheimer's, nor did her sister! Since we can create a different life by MAKING ourselves go out and walk in clean air while breathing deeply, eating properly, etc., creating and choosing HEALTH over a slow torturous death, let's do it! I know that when I walk and eat properly, my head becomes clearer, enabling me to do more in the house, at writing, and at my job.

On TV in "1999" they said 4,000,000 people have Alzheimer's disease. It has to be more because how many have not yet been to a doctor? There is no cure for Alzheimer's! Scientists should work with me and/or other spiritual healers IN PEOPLE'S HOMES for a cure, so you will see what they are *all* about. Remember Alzheimer's people "SEE THINGS."

July 7,1999: Doctors have a vaccine that MIGHT fight against Alzheimer's. They don't know if it will cure dementia, or if it will have an adverse reaction on people because it was *tested* on MICE. (So what's the use?) It might be ready in five years. An *instant* cure enables people to heal their *body* but I hope their doctors tell them that unless they also heal their *mind* and *soul,* they can create that same disease again and /OR illness in another part of their body.

Later in January 1999, I had the pleasure of meeting a woman who is 102 years old. She doesn't need or use reading glasses or Depends. She eats butter and dessert every day and has never taken a vitamin.

"I've never had an ache or pain in my whole life," she told me. I saw *no spots* on her at all! She has a smile that lights up a room and my soul. She never has a negative word to say about anything or anyone, and still talks about how wonderful her mother and father were. She is definitely "in the moment."

One morning she asked me, "Is the sun out?"

"No, it's not out today," I answered.

She smiled and said, "Well, I guess we'll just have to take it then."

***

Everything IS *connected.*

Let's talk more about Christina: She was sick for about seven years, off and on. She had gone into remission for a few years after a mastectomy. The last couple of years were agony for her and everyone else. She never admitted to me or even to her husband that she was dying. I wouldn't admit it to myself. I drove almost an hour each way to help her at home, and to take the two youngest children out for the day, so that she could get some rest. It was also sad seeing the children's pain. They would never verbalize it, which was a continuation of the circle. Somehow, and on some level of existence, being there helping her, rather than hiding from her felt right. Not that I could "feel" much of anything at all. At this time my dilemma was that my mother was sick, my father was in a nursing home, and I only had one day a week off from work to help everyone. I would drive almost an hour after work to take my mother to the nursing home, to see and help my father. Each time we had to go shopping because his personal belongings were mysteriously disappearing from the nursing home.

I was recently told a story about an elderly woman who had been living in a nursing home for a long time. Each day she would take her small diamond ring out to hold and remember her husband and all the good times they had. When asked by her family if she wanted them to take it home for safe keeping, she answered no, it was all she had left in her life. Within a week the ring was stolen. The next day, she died. The ring, which held her soul, had been taken away. At a later date, my mother was in a nursing home, and her diamond wedding band was stolen from her hand. No one in a position of authority did anything about it. How nursing home employees are allowed to get away with stealing jewelry and clothing from their patients, or other abuses such as punching or raping helpless patients, in this day and age is *beyond* me, my friends and my family.

A girl, in her twenties, said to me, "Don't worry about anything." The only thing that worries me is people like her who think that way. If you're being abused, someone with that attitude won't help you. "I don't *worry*, I put my thoughts into action!!!" TALK IS CHEAP.

February 22, 1999: Today on television there was an 800 number to call to report abuse in nursing homes. Check with your local city hall for the number. Don't let anyone get away with this horrendous abuse.

As a result of Christina's, my father's and mother's illnesses, I had very little time for dealing with my own problems in life. As I re-read these notes in January 1999, I ask myself, "Would I spend as much time helping all three as I did?" The answer is, "YES!" Only I would take more time to walk, eat better, relax and meditate for my own personal well-being. 5/99 It's easier said than done, although I shower twice a day, I have to put time aside a month in advance to take a long, hot bath. I am on a mission.

One day Christina asked me for a ride to her doctor's appointment. I said I would, but I couldn't help wondering why she asked me to take her, when she had never asked me before. I drove her to the hospital in Boston, where her doctor was waiting in a cold, stark white, insipid examination room. As she sat on an intimidating short stool with a flimsy hospital gown on, she looked up at her doctor meekly, took a deep breath, and after hesitating for what seemed a lifetime, she asked, "How long do I have to live?" The air was no longer in the room for me and time did not exist...he did not answer. After what seemed to be an eternity, she mustered up the strength to ask him one last time, "How long do I have to live??" Again, he did not answer. I couldn't believe the insensitivity of this man, couldn't he see and feel how hard that question was for her? I lost my Irish temper and in a strong voice said, "She asked you a perfectly *valid* question. Why don't you answer her?" In that moment I didn't even know where my strength came from, because it was the first time she admitted in front of me that she was dying. Of course it was strength from God.

The doctor nastily replied, "I don't know!"

"You must have SOME idea, SOME range of time," I insisted angrily.

He replied sarcastically, "I don't have a *crystal* ball."

Christina finally had no cute little sayings to make this all go away. Had this been a few months earlier, when she was feeling better, Christina would have said something like: *"Maybe we should buy him some crystal balls. He really could use them."*

My numbness and sadness were mixed with anger and frustration, only to be totally taken over by rage. So much for BEDSIDE manner. He's the same doctor who didn't help cure Christina's mother of cancer. There seems to be a cloud over his office. On our long, sad, confused ride home, Christina decided that she wanted Chinese food. It's a strange feeling when you're with someone who's dying. Your whole view of the world changes. Everything seems to be so different. I would have done anything in my power to get her anything she wanted...although my power was quickly diminishing. Every restaurant we went into did not appeal to her.

"We'll get it next time," she said sadly. But there was no next time. Christina died a couple of weeks later, which was one week after my father passed away, around Halloween.

My father's and Christina's suffering is over. Mine, to some extent, is still continuing. I'm very happy that Christina has no more chemotherapy, no more ignorant doctor to put up with and no more pain of any sort. I know she'll come back to check up on her children.

A week before she passed over, she was still "pleasing" people. One way was by going to a party at her husband's club. I went along not only to drive her to and from the event, but to allow her to inconspicuously lean on me physically and spiritually. You have to give her credit for being strong-willed "for others," but her body told the *truth*!

At Christina's wake there were some of the most beautiful flowers I have ever seen. There was a huge heart made out of green carnations that kept silent vigil over her body's eternal bed. I knew that if anyone could come to her own wake in spirit, to see who would show up, it would be Christina. I kept pensively waiting for a sign from her. I looked around for the large spray of carnations with the one lonely red rose in the center, which I had purchased. I found the arrangement at her feet staring down at me, and as I stared back, I noticed the rose was beginning to move very slowly. As I looked at it wistfully, it appeared to be turning brown. I looked away and rubbed my eyes. My first reaction was: I'm going to get my money back on that rose. I looked back only to see it continuing to bend over at a faster rate. It took my breath away. If someone in my spiritual class had mentioned the rose, I would have instantly cleared up what was happening, but I was sitting there alone and in denial. Finally, it was so obvious that I admitted to myself that it was Christina touching it and not the poor quality of the rose. By now the rose was totally dead. I should have been happy she had gotten in touch with me, but to me the rose now symbolized our once living friendship.

"Coincidentally," our friend Yvonne was attending a family wake in the *next room* of the *same* funeral parlor in "Southie," on the *exact same day* as Christina's wake. Yvonne had been introduced to her husband years before while in a small tavern in "Southie," by Christina, who had dated his brother. Naturally, Yvonne came by to pay her respects, but it meant that she would be unable to come to the church and cemetery with me and a few other friends the next day. I could have used all the support I could get. I think it's the priest's job to make you cry, through soft, loving words, almost as if to wash and cleanse the soul. This priest knew Christina well and was openly upset. The church to me is the biggest test of all and I very rarely pass it. It's just so devastating… mostly for the living because hopefully, the spirit has gone to the light of God, "The Light of Life." Everyone should be educated on how to help send souls over to God's protection so they may rest in peace.

Within a couple of weeks after the funeral, I helped Christina's husband with her belongings. He mentioned that some of the dresses were borrowed and had to be returned to friends and family. I have a pretty turquoise dress and matching earrings which Christina gave to me. She said someone *gave* them to her. I offered to return them, but he said they really had been *given* to Christina. We came across Christina's very worn flannel bathrobe. As her daughter hugged it, she asked if she could keep it.

"Yes," her father said.

About a month later, the seven-year old daughter brought the bathrobe back to her father saying, "I think you can have it back *now*." I, on the other hand, still have Christina's almost empty Chanel No. 5 perfume bottle, and ear rings. I guess you have to be seven years old to know when to let go.

In February, a few months after Christina passed, I went to a spiritualist church and received a wonderful message from a man I had never met before. He said, "You are going through difficult times. You are determined to make things work.

Keep the tender part of you alive. Keep up a good fight. There is strength in numbers. Things will work out. You have two children around you (Christina's youngest). One will do very well. You will be proud to be a part of their lives. The woman with cancer comes and touches you and promises that she will help you in any way she can."

Tears started streaming down my face. The woman who came with me, and did not even know Christina, cried too. Even strangers in the church were crying. Everyone could feel that the message was true.

A couple of weeks later I attended a different spiritualist church and was happy to receive another message; this time from a woman I didn't know. (This was very unusual for me because I seldom receive spiritual messages at service.) She said, "Lighten up on yourself. You are *not* losing someone, and she is not losing either. Stay above water. Someone is around you that you love. A woman from the spirit side is here. She smoked a lot and did not have much of a voice left before she passed. She wants you to know she loves you." That was the last thing Christina weakly whispered to me from her hospital bed.

To some extent, I'm still in a fog of denial. Christina was so good to everyone. I guess it was easier than looking at her own pain and problems, as it is for many of us. Some pain runs too deep, like the blood through our veins and hearts. My pain, sorrow and emptiness are subsiding, little by little, as the years go by. My mother's Irish strength had said to me, "How *dare* you cry! You *have* to be strong for your friend and her children."

Now I have to be strong for *me*.
I love you too.

Take good care of yourself!!!

As I reminisce today, it's hard for me to believe she's gone. I see that everywhere I turn in my past Christina is there. Long ago, I was between office jobs, so I took a job driving 766 children in a school car in Boston where Christina worked. We also waited tables together in such places as executive restaurants in town, a sub shop in South Boston and the Continental Lounge in Dorchester. I adopted an extraordinary Siamese cat named Marco because of Christina...my mother loved Marco so much that when I finally moved out of the house, Mom said, "the *cat* has to stay." Christina and I smoked, danced, went to beaches together, doubled dated at drive-ins, and met in the lunch room at the "Woody." We lost two good friends to Vietnam, Mark and Harry. We used to walk together a lot before we got our driver's licenses. We went horseback riding; once was enough for her. We also rode on the back of motorcycles with a respected club called "The Road Runners." Once in awhile, we would pile into my father's wonderful, old "55" Chevy, outside the donut shop, and talk for hours, or go for a cruise. We all thought time was on our side! I *really missed* that car when he *surprised* me with a huge, all power Buick LeSabre. My dad made me pay for ALL the repairs on both cars, since I was sixteen years old.

I must confess I have another little story about fixing up a quiet, religious, choir-singing, sewing, knitting, homebody named Samantha. Pretty Samantha only weighed about one hundred pounds soaking wet and had long, gorgeous, natural light blond hair. Samantha had just bought a brand new "1967" powder blue Ford Mustang. She went on a blind double date with me and my date, Richard. Her date was a nice biker named Jim from another distinguished club called "The Devil's Disciples."

My date and I were in the back seat of her new car, while her date, Jim, was in the front passenger seat. We were in her beautiful car only a second, when Jim took the longest cigarette I have ever seen in my life out of his leather coat pocket. Before I could get the words out of my slow mouth, he proceeded to light it. Well, Sam, who drives staring straight ahead with both hands in a death grip on the wheel, did not even skip a beat. Without looking, she swung her arm, and as quiet, little Samantha yelled from the corner of her stern, set mouth, "NO SMOKING IN MY CAR," she proceeded to (accidentally, of course) belt him right across the mouth, bending the oversized cigarette in half. Now, *Big Jim*, the bikie, cautiously, and with much confusion, very slowly and methodically turned his head, eyes first, toward Samantha. His mouth was hanging open with this huge broken butt looking like an upside down V stuck to his bottom lip, with a terribly baffled look on his shocked face. Richard and I were laughing so hard we couldn't speak, and tears were streaming down our faces! Finally, in the restaurant Jim took the same pack out of his pocket, hesitated, looked at Sam and half jokingly asked her if he could smoke NOW?? We all laughed again. That was our topic of discussion for most of the evening and now for most of our lives. Jim was a good sport and a true gentleman. To be honest, Samantha was as quiet as I used to be, so I would say and do little things to bring her out. (But I never expected "out that far.") I don't know WHY she never went on a blind date with any more of my friends again. I'm sure there are some bikies I wouldn't go out with, like anything else there are good and bad in every group.

In those days smoking was "in." Today it isn't. I'm grateful they took cigarette commercials off television. That was instrumental in my finally quitting after so many tries.

Once, Sam and I were cooking spaghetti at my parent's home. We looked on in astonishment as the top of the spaghetti, which was leaning against the rim of the pot, began to turn black - then burst into flames. At the exact same moment we looked at each other, something clicked between us like E.S.P., and we screamed together, "Quick, get the scissors!!" I never said, "sewing" Samantha could *cook!*

MY little story about cooking is: I had some friends over for dinner. As I put my beautiful stainless steel pans, which had 24 carat gold-coated handles and glass lids with gold knobs, on the burner... it was as if E. F. Hutton had spoken.

The silence was so scary that I carefully and slowly turned to see what had happened. Shirley and Samantha, among other friends, were staring at the pans with their mouths agape.

Then Shirley as if in a dream, softly said, "Look at those *beautiful* pans, she doesn't even cook." What was stranger for me is, I had only known Shirley for about a year, and the only thing I ever saw Shirley cook was "Paul Newman!" Although, I did see her making ice cubes one day!!

Sam, looking stunned, said, "There's not even a WATER stain on them." Even today, Samantha and I laugh about all those WONDERFUL memories, but I was TOTALLY surprised at everyone's reaction.

My motorcycle friends were protective of me. For instance, one day a white man was coming from the trolley stop near my home at 10 A.M. I thought that was strange because normally people on their way to work, as I was, would be heading toward the trolley. I also had a bad feeling about him, so I was on my guard. As he approached me, he made eye contact, then quickly looked down at my feet. He then, in a fast motion, came in front of me and tried to grab me. I was prepared and had my arms up in front of me. Immediately, I started to fight him off, catching him off guard, I pushed him backwards. He kept apologizing as he ran to his car, which was waiting with the engine running near the corner of the intersection.

If that happened today I would call the police, although I didn't do so at the time. I've since learned the importance of doing so. I wasn't brought up to come from behind the curtain when something was wrong. I told some of my motorcycle friends, who were like brothers to me, about the incident. They drove up and down my street for months around 10 A.M., to protect me as I went to work. In those days, women couldn't even wear nice pantsuits to work (or church), or I would have accepted a ride to the station with them. I was blessed to have met them on my journey. Thank you all! When my body dies I want a lot of motorcycles to attend - so I can have one last ride before I go home.

But I digress. Christina never traveled much except when she and I went to Laconia, NH, for a motorcycle race weekend. We met a group of friends up there, and had some innocent fun. We were in a car accident on the way up. I saw my life flash before my eyes, then I *passed* OUT cold. I ended up with several stitches on my nose. I had been in the middle of the back seat and out of six people I had been the only one injured.

Once we went to Cape Cod, and partied at a cottage called Bunratty's in the Falmouth area with Dick Doherty and some newer friends of mine, such as Kevin and Eddie. Of course everyone slept on beach chairs, in the tub, on the couch, or slept five to a bed, including a water bed, leaving the original renter out in the cold. We don't have fun like *that* anymore!!

By our late twenties we slowed the pace of our lifestyle, Christina more than me, because by then she was married and had started her family. She went out to Bingo and played the daily numbers a lot. I wasn't into that, although I went to Bingo with her a few times just before she *passed over*. I couldn't concentrate the way she could, because I was in a daze of denial over her "now obvious" illness. I don't know how she could concentrate on all those cards playing Bingo and winning. She even helped me with my *two* cards. Now I stay in more than I've ever done before, because I no longer have a "Christina" to pry me out of my house, or is it because of my spiritual journey?

***

January 1999:It's literally been years since I've been out at night with the girls.

Three of us decided to go out to dinner. One girl, whom I had just met that evening, attracted two married men whom she knew, to the table.

One of the men immediately and intensely stared right through my eyes.

I asked him, "So, how long have you been psychic?"

Being a bit high, he slurred, "Twenty years." Not knowing me, he went on to ask, "Did you know you can create your destiny?"

I thought to myself, "You mean like two sober, single men???" Why didn't I think of that BEFORE I left the house?

He went on to say he didn't believe in dreams.

I said, "I do. In Egypt they believe dreams are our reality."

He replied, "I don't know that much about Egypt."

I said, "A friend of mine told me that in Europe, about 3000 years ago, tribes of people were living in huts made of dirt, grass and twigs, wearing animal skins, drinking from animal horns, and eating with their hands. While at the same time, Pharaohs living in Egypt were so much more advanced, that they were living in luxurious palaces, with brilliantly painted walls, and grand statues of gods and goddesses. Women wore garments of finely woven fabrics and used cosmetics to beautify themselves. They slept in "bedrooms," swam in pools and ate and drank from pottery. Don't forget the grandeur of the pyramids and the great sphinx. Where did they get all of their information from so many years ago?"

I asked him, "Do you believe in the moon controlling people as it does the tides, etc., as people's bodies are composed of mostly water?"

He replied, "Yes, but the other planets don't control us."

I said to myself, "He OBVIOUSLY never dated a GEMINI, TWO personalities! Oh well, the night was not a total loss." At this point I needed to hear about CREATING MY DESTINY again, to help me through this VERY LONG journey of channeling and writing this book.

Today, in retrospect, I can't believe the snow storms my old friends and I would travel in, as though they were nothing. That's really being in the moment. Today, if they forecast snow for tomorrow, I won't go out tonight. I still remember my mother's warnings about weather: "Don't go out," or "Be careful," "Come home early," "Dress warm," and "Where are your boots??" The weather forecasters are just as bad at over-exaggerating storms which usually don't show up. I've learned that the weather people still make a lot of mistakes even though their instruments are more advanced today than they were in the "60's"and "70's." Or just maybe an angel prayed for the sun to come out in place of the rain that day. Too much power and energy is given to storms that never show up. Let's pray for the sun, and calm loving weather instead.

Still reminiscing: A friend of mine, Patty, from junior high, whose brother I dated platonically, married Christina's husband's brother, who was also named Pat. No, we didn't fix them up. We hardly even knew him at that time. More patterns, circles and connections in the crossroads of our lives! Remember, this was all happening in a big city with "tons" of people, yet it seems the world keeps getting smaller and smaller.

In our early teens, Christina, Yvonne and I ended up in a little fender bender. We went to the Boston City Hospital to be checked out. My head was bothering me so much that the doctor strapped me onto a gurney and told me not to move, because this could be a SERIOUS injury! I was going to be X-rayed soon. So there I was, lying on this stupid, small gurney, with no blanket and just a flimsy johnny on, and I heard Christina and Yvonne (Larry and Moe), giggling and running through the hospital halls in their johnnies looking for me. To my dismay, they found me and started pushing my gurney "full speed ahead" down the corridors, taking the corners on two wheels. I was holding on to the johnny with one hand and to the side of the mattress with the other, trying to keep my head still, and at the same time, screaming at the top of my lungs. After chasing us down a few corridors, the nurse finally rescued me. They were scolded and chased back to their rooms to wait for their X-rays. Ahh, the good old days!! Two perplexing shadows showed up on Christina's X-rays. The doctors called her mother to come to the hospital. Naturally everyone was *very concerned.* As it turned out, Christina, being extremely modest, had refused to remove her underwear. The shadows were her bra clasps. I have never seen Christina's mother so angry. Of course, we thought the end results were very funny! Isn't it ironic and sad that years later those marks came back, and this time helped to kill her.

Yet, another childhood friend, this time from grammar school, whom I introduced to Christina, was Linda Carlson. I had known her since living in my first home, a triple-decker, across the street from the rail-road tracks on Norwell Street, Dorchester, where we attended elementary school together. It was told to me that the scarecrow in the Wizard of Oz, named Ray Bolger, was also born on Norwell Street. I called the Public Library, they could only confirm that Ray was born in Dorchester. We call it O.F.D., "Originally From Dorchester." It was this street where I rescued my first cat. I said to some *very* tall bullies, please don't do that, after some convincing they let him go, and he ran quickly away. Anyway, Linda is the kind of friend who would literally give you the shirt off her back. Linda became engaged to Christina's brother. Doesn't it seem we were all together in another place and time and planned these meetings?

One day Linda pulled quickly up into our driveway on Adams Street, leaving her car running and the door flung open. (4/99: It JUST occurred to me that Linda is the only one I still ran around with from the old neighborhood.)

She ran into my family's living room, out of breath saying, "Donna, I had this awful dream last night." Linda was trembling so much she could hardly speak.

She went on to say, "I dreamt that something awful happened to me and my ex-boyfriend, George (of five years). We somehow ended up together for eternity."

I asked, "How could that happen? You're engaged to someone else and so is he."

She shakily replied, "I don't know, but it was like a nightmare, it was so real."

This was very disconcerting to me, because after knowing Linda all these years, I had never seen her like this before. As a matter of fact, she was the most stable one of us all. Linda had a good, permanent job and drove a brand new big car. I made her promise me she would never go out with George again - *EVER*, so we could be assured that nothing bad would happen to her. She promised. This was another sad example of me not knowing how to use my abilities at this young time of my life, and how to help poor Linda, or anyone else for that matter, who sought me out to tell me their problems, pains and secrets, as people usually do.

Within a month I received a call at work from Christina saying Linda was dead, and George would probably not make it through the night. Linda and George had gone for one last ride together just to say good-bye, before they married other people. They were in a freak car accident. His compact car careened out of control, rolled over several times in the Southbound lane of Route 128, and then finally over the embankment.

Evidently, when Linda calmed down from her nightmare, she must have let what she thought to be reality, slowly creep in, thinking and rationalizing that *there was nothing to her dream.* After all, if Linda had prayed for an answer whether or not to go out with George that day, I'm sure she would have gotten a feeling of: "I'd better not go today. Thanks anyway." We were all around twenty years old. It was a very traumatic and hard lesson for us all. Someday we'll *all* be together!

Soon after completing this chapter, I had a very real dream of being in a car accident with a friend while on an exit ramp from Route 128. Instead of her taking a right, it was almost as though someone else took control of the car, and accelerated full speed ahead straight across the street into a pole directly in front of us. I looked up with a gasp cut short, as blackness quickly descended on me. It was so realistic, I sat up wide awake wondering what to do about it. I haven't been in a car with that person since. I can now see how Linda could have possibly changed her mind, or ignored her dream, because within a week of MY dream, my friend and I casually talked about going shopping in the same area of the accident in my life-like dream. However, I thought of Linda and quickly changed my mind...but what if I had forgotten, or been in denial that the dream "could" be valid?

May 1999: This book, but especially this chapter has taken on a life of its own!

Donna and God: There are a lot of other stories that stem from these stories. All of these true stories are cleansing lessons for our minds, bodies and souls. Once in a while I do feel sorry for myself because of the hard life I live, but now I realize that I'm to *embrace them wholly* with a smile and no fear. By *not* doing that, I've made my predestined life even more difficult. Always remember: Sorrow gives Satan power. I have angels, spirits, Christ, Mother Mary, Michael and God, who come to me from heaven's side as "Holy Ghosts," ("Holy Spirits"). I also have earthbound souls with bodies, who are my disciples. They assist me and move around to also help others like yourself. *Open your heart and soul to them - let them in, God.*

Even when I think there is no one here with me, I'm then proven to be wrong. Another example besides the last paragraph is: I had been up all night with a new kitten I had rescued. She turned out to be very sick. I was begging for sleep, but as my head hit the pillow around 5 A.M., totally exhausted, my huge female cat, Bartet, being very jealous, picked this time to show it by viciously growling (which I had never heard her do before or since) at our new, tiny kitten, who by the way, was minding her own business. I was in that nice space just before you fall into that wonderful deep sleep. My heart and mind were saying, "I have to get up before Bartet kills her," but my body was not moving. "The spirit was willing but the flesh was weak." ,All of a sudden, as Bartet was still growling, I heard this sweet, angelic voice near Bartet, slowly and softly saying, "Now, now, everything is going to be all right." And then again, even more softly, "Everything is going to be *all right*." Almost as if she were patting Bartet. The minute she spoke, Bartet stopped growling at the kitten, named Angel. I carefully opened my eyes a bit, but saw no one. I begged her to keep talking just so I could hear and enjoy more of her beautiful, harmonious voice, but she did not. It was obvious to me that I could finally go to sleep.

The next day, Angel and Bartet played nicely together, as all sisters should.

Chapter 3

A Gift from God

February 1999: (This will give you an idea of how much was interjected.) We are now going back to the *original* writings of 1995. The next prayer mentioned is from chapter 1, page 1. It's obvious God and Christina wanted Chapter 2 interjected.

***

1995: I've had problems all my life, but even *more* started just before that prayer. Then it *all* hit the fan. I was getting *no* sleep. I had to put my eighteen-year-old cat Yo-Yo to sleep. A lot of you know how *that* feels. A woman who called me her sister, (figuratively speaking) stabbed me in the back. Another lesson for me, I guess. Why is it whenever someone is guilty of something, it's *always* THE OTHER *person. It's always* everyone else's fault Those are lies to yourself, to preserve your own sanity, God says. Lies keep *you* FROM *your own sanity!!!* Anyway, that was only part of my April 22nd birthday, also Earth Day, present. I was *trying* to sleep on my couch which was like a re-birthing for me, a crib, if you will. Instead, I've been awake writing for four nights and five days. (Which turned out to be a lot more nights than that with only a *few* hours sleep. Once written, the book still needed to be typed, edited, then printed.) 2/1999: If I had known in 1995 it was going to take this long I would have been VERY discouraged.

On the third day of *troubles*, I was extremely depressed and wanted to give up; just then a bird perched on my wrought iron fence. My four-year-old cat, who had been a stray and usually pounces, just sat and looked on in astonishment. The bird was looking back and forth at both of us for some time with something in his beak. In disbelief, I *ran* to the sliding door. The bird placed a green plant with a *large* root system *still intact* on my balcony floor, looked directly at me again and, *after* making sure I saw the present, the bird flew away.

***Bartet** showing interest in the gift. The light in this picture happens to be where the bird left the present. I quickly placed stones and soil in this Howard mug, then later I transplanted it into a clay pot.*

A GIFT FROM GOD came to me very clearly. "Don't give up!" WE see your pain, *don't give up*. It came to me at a time, when in addition to all the other problems I was having, I was feeling *excruciating* PAIN in my lower legs, just like when I was around four years old. *Then, we* called it "growing pains."

Now God says to me, "It's fear of an unsettling future." God says, "*Give the plant back*, give it back *to the earth*. Let go of the past. Go forward with love and trust *that* EVERYTHING IS WHERE IT SHOULD BE!" I needed it so badly, I planted it, left it in my home and loved *it to death*. Every time *I* looked at it, *I* felt happiness. *It* felt like dying. *It* needed to be free, but I needed it so much to make *me* happy, to make *me feel* as though I'm not alone in my pain. Every time I looked at it I realized that it was TRULY *a gift from God*. God says to me, "Mothers and fathers, husbands and wives, people and their old pets, does it feel familiar? We have to fill that hole within us." The plant was *so sad* that it died but *still* I kept it trapped here in my house, SAFE *from the outside*. *Finally*, after too long a time, I took it back outside under a tree and planted it in the ground where it belonged, but it was gone forever now. I killed it! Then I felt *no one* had the right to take *it* away from me, my stubbornness and ego. *It* was *mine!* Because I've had problems all my life, I cherished this gift as my little ray of light coming through from the other side and I had to give it up again. I would have it today, to look at under that tree, if it weren't for *my own* selfishness. Now it *belongs* to no one---because of me.

We do hold on too much, DON'T WE! Until WE DRAIN *the life out of things*. People and pets, *we* kill them one way or the other, WE *kill them*. Much in the same way, we are killing this world. It's just a *small* example of *my whole life*. I've had the same problems over and over again.

God says to me, "STOP THE CIRCLES!"

It doesn't seem fair that everywhere I look there is pain and sorrow, God. Here I am, God, help me. I don't want to play anymore. I'm as LOW as I can go. Help me to understand *this* life. What is *it?* How do I find *IT?* I *command* in the *name of Jesus Christ,* so make it be, and so IT *begins.*

Chapter 4

Still Learning

It took me five days of no sleep and heartbreaking "coincidences" to get me to this low, open, unearthly point in my life. I was missing my eighteen-year-old cat so much that I foster parented three kittens in hopes of finding them good homes. It's always good to keep at least two pets together so they can share warmth and companionship. Of course, I became so attached to the three kittens, I would have loved to have kept *all three,* or at the very least one. Then they all, became sick. (Coincidences again?)

My four-year-old cat, Bartet, was not pleased with any of them to begin with and wanted them all out of *her* home. (This was just before I had my Angel kitten.) I was getting ready to leave and bring them back to my acquaintance, Diane, who runs a "no-kill" shelter, when I looked down at the kitchen floor, where I had been feeding them, and noticed a green stone in the middle of the cat mat. It was a stone which had been in the living room on a table. One of the kittens had left it where they ate as a thank you. An outdoor cat might, unfortunately, bring a mouse or something else home which is very cruel. These indoor cats express themselves with what they have access to.

Well *this* devastated me. How much more do I have to endure? They knew they were leaving, and I had to put them in the cat carrier. Their sad little eyes looking up at me from the box and one of them fighting hard to get out. God, this was another tough lesson. It was like yet *another* death to me.

As I was driving back with the kittens, crying all the way to Boston, I was thinking, "There has to be an easier way to live in this sad world." One thing after another. Diane, to whom I returned the kittens, kept them many weeks, not wanting to give them to *just* ANYONE. She later told me that a few minutes after I dropped them off, they were playing, running and scampering around the room. *I should be so*

RESILIENT! However, if you have a pet for a long time, and give it away, it could die of a broken heart, unless you are abusive, in which case *everyone* would be *glad* to leave you.

-This is one of three kittens, which all looked alike. He was holding the green stone-

Definition of resilient: The ability to withstand strain without being personally affected or injured. Also able to recover quickly from depression and maintain high spirits.

What a joke! I was NONE of *these*. Why can't *I* let go? Why can't *I* start playing immediately after something *depressing happens to me? Now what was I to do? NOW* what was I to do? I was sad and tired beyond belief because, in addition to everything else, the past couple of nights before they left, the kittens and I had been chasing the biggest black ants I have ever seen. They were mysteriously climbing up the side of my building to my top floor apartment. When I asked others in the building about the ants, they had no idea what I was talking about. My reply was, "What do you think, they are bypassing everyone else's apartment and just coming up to mine?" When in fact, that was EXACTLY what was happening.

After a few nights it was still going on. It seemed like hundreds of ants had come in and more were still coming. I must confess, I said a little prayer that at least ONE *other person* in the building would get ants so something would finally be done, and my neighbor would stop thinking that I could possibly be crazy. It was really getting out of hand. The ants were EVERYWHERE in the apartment and I was praying for no bad *karma*, you know, *what goes around comes around*, from that little prayer. As a result of my prayer, the next day the head trustee's wife told me she was grossed out when she stepped on a very large ant in her kitchen while *she was barefoot*. *Then* things started happening, the trustees talked about getting bug powder and exterminators.

That night as I was getting out of the tub, *I* stepped on a *huge* ant, so I guess that was *my bad karma* coming back to haunt me because *it felt* AWFUL!

Chapter 5

Donna Marie Talking with God

Totally exhausted, this prayer came to me to say. After I had said, "*Please, God*, I need the strength to get me through these days and nights." The prayer was,

Here I am Lord, I am ready. Teach me. Let me learn to love and know what this veil is that has been covering my face, my soul, and my mind all of my life.

PLEASE HELP!!!

Donna Marie: "I need at least a couple of hours sleep tonight. *Please*!"

God: "*Sleep is for common people!!!*"

Donna Marie: "Tell that to my human body!" At this point I was more wired than tired. That was meant in jest, coming from my Dorchester citified upbringing. God's messages and lessons are coming to me through birds, kittens and now ants. I'm afraid to ask, "*What next!?*" I did sleep for a little while. What was strange about it is, my cat who weighs seventeen pounds and *never* sleeps with me on the couch, slept with me that evening. What got me up at 1 A.M. was an *ant* crawling on my thigh. I guess God didn't want me to sleep again this night. Well *that's* okay, I'll get up and see what *lessons* are next. Well it was definitely a "wake-up" call. Awake again, now I'm angry. "What are you doing to me? Haven't I suffered enough in this awful life? Just take me over to the other side. I'm ready now. There is nothing here for me. I'm tired, bored and physically sick."(I had been having these problems with my stomach and back since before the start of this book.)

"Help me understand what *this* is. I'm horrified at these ants, angry and tired."

I called William, my landlord, the following morning. He wasn't using his house on Cape Cod, and offered it to me for as long as I wanted. Even though he's allergic to my cat, he said I could take her with me so he could put some ant powder around my apartment/his condominium, and that way Bartet would not be harmed by it. I could have some rest finally, and HOPEFULLY some sleep. The minute I committed to going to the Cape, I saw NO MORE ANTS. The head trustee's wife said her ants had disappeared too. I thought, "Well, this is good. I don't have to go down to the Cape. I can stay home. I can get some sleep here in my own bed." You guessed it! The ants came back! All right, ALL RIGHT I'M GOING. I'm going to the Cape. Even though I wasn't leaving for a few days, I started to pack to prove my sincerity. Again the ants stopped coming into my apartment.

I had not put *it* all together yet, but it was Saturday and I was in a euphoric state all day. I had connected to something directly on the other side. I was like a zombie but *awake* at the same time. I figured if I went to the *air show* where "The Blue Angels" were flying, it would really put me over the edge. So *I went!* What did I have to lose? A girl from church came with her young son. He was making me very nervous by repeating questions, not hearing, not listening, confused, lost. Oh, my God! My childhood has come back to haunt me! He and I both have *attention deficit disorder* although I believe he had a more serious case than I.

I was becoming *very aware*, the less sleep I got, the more aware and in touch I became. *It* was starting to hit me and come *into me*. Everywhere I looked today, I saw my childhood. This time I will take a good look at it and cleanse it. One of the most important things I ask is, *"Why do I keep going in circles, God?"* I'm getting dizzy and sick, and feeling old and tired. I keep making the SAME *mistakes* over and over and over again. The more I saw, the more like a sponge I was. I was even starting to recognize and *feel* what animals need. Yes, they also have needs. If you're not meeting those needs, you shouldn't have a pet. Many dogs are killed when their owners tie them to bumpers, forget about them and drive off dragging the dogs behind. It's true. Sad and stupid, but true. Whether you have a good memory or not, *don't tie your dog to any part of your vehicle,* or people will think your lights are on, but nobody's home.

I also met a girl at the air show who went from riding in the back of a truck to being under its wheels. She's now retarded and has lost movement in her left side as a result of the accident. So, keep your friends, family and pets up front WITH YOU. We all see too many trucks on the main roads and highways going *well over the speed limit,* with dogs and/or kids bouncing almost out of the back into OUR laps. Please, call the police and report them. Don't try to deal with the situation yourself. Make it a law in EVERY STATE that no living thing be allowed to ride in the back of a truck. Some places already have it. I smile at the men who have their dogs proudly sitting up front with them. "1999": Now they want you to have seat belts for pets INSIDE your vehicles, yet they're still endangering pets lives, and people in the cars behind and around them, by keeping them in the *back* of their trucks.

God and Donna: "SELFISHNESS!" Everything that *I (people) wanted* and *needed,* for *ME, not* for *it, or them.* The closer to God you are, the closer to animals, children and trees you are. *YOU are the universe, listen to the way of the Lord.*

Chapter 6

My Wish to be Awake

We do blame things on what happened yesterday, *then* we want to be responsible for our own decisions NOW as adults. But this insight was like seeing *a road map* of *my childhood by street, and by neighborhood,* placed over one another, and my *problems/lessons ON* EVERY STREET *repeating* themselves. They were there to *wake me up*! I was forced to fight physically and mentally all of my life, going back also to the A.D.D., Attention Deficit Disorder. They didn't have a name for it back then except for, stupid, unconscious, and when are you going to wake up? I also grew up on the wrong side of the tracks (*whatever that* means) in Boston. It's a good thing I didn't know it was "the wrong side of the tracks," because most of the time, I loved it.

Most of my friends today tell me not to mention my A.D.D. because I come across as *being intelligent* and having a lot of common sense, so no one would ever know. When I was younger I used the ESSENCE, the flow, the rhythm of what people were saying to figure out what the big word they used meant. I could even then USE that word eventually in the right context still not knowing exactly what it meant. "Context" is an easy, good example, it just popped into my head and was spelled properly as I automatically typed, as if someone was helping me. A savant must feel the same way. I trusted and *felt* that it was right but I never knew its EXACT meaning, just the essence of it. A.D.D. was such a big part of my confusion as a child that I can't sweep it under the rug. It still follows me almost as much today as it did when I was a child, only I'm not being embarrassed by being tested in school. A.D.D. to me, is like once in awhile someone gives you a phone number in the wrong sequence such as, 61712-3456--7. Then I have to *strain* to TRY to understand *it, and* ask them to repeat it till they say the sentence in a "simplistic" way for me. Sometimes, if it goes on for too long, my head actually hurts, as if on overload and I have to stop all together. Sometimes I just GET IT! It wasn't until writing this book that I finally absorbed, and almost totally understood sentence structure. That's something I never would have admitted years ago. The reason I said "ALMOST totally" is that everyone, even teachers and librarians TODAY, are confusing me by having different opinions on where to place commas, etc. Samantha has been helping me A LOT with this. Thanks Sam! I have only known for a couple of years about A.D.D., and only two people have told me not to use it as an excuse. In looking at what they said to me though, I didn't say IT until around the fourth time I asked them to explain something to me in an easier, slower way, like 1-2-3. They said they also have A.D.D., but I said, you've been doing this same paper work for twenty-five years, I just started. They were just not meant to teach, but it was a missed opportunity to help. I hope that reading *my* story helps others.

There were a lot of children of different colors and nationalities to play with where I lived in Dorchester, some were near my age, thank God, because my two brothers and sisters were a lot older than I.

My oldest sister was around twenty-one years old when I was born. My brothers, *ironically,* were studying to be teachers and called me stupid. My Irish Catholic mother was ALWAYS praying for her child to be taken care of, leaving *me in the hands of God.* I was changing schools often and was made to go to special reading classes. It was embarrassing, coming out of that classroom. I still hate September because I remember the fear of "Please don't call on me." How could we forget the old, stale, dry, sometimes toxic smells of school, the taste of school, the heat of the school room, and the homework! I'd like to forget those *soggy* peanut butter and jelly sandwiches made on white bread, which would get all mushy and stick to the roof of my mouth, the smell of my lunch box when I first opened it and having to drink warm milk when I was LACTOSE intolerant. Of course, they also didn't discover "that" until another forty years too late for me and many others from my childhood. Someone I met did his own little unscientific survey and discovered that everyone he has spoken to that has A.D.D. also is lactose intolerant. I wonder if they have yeast problems which also fogs the mind. Who knows? On TV, in June of 1999, someone mentioned lead paint poisoning has some of the same symptoms as A.D.D.

January 23, 1999: This alone was worth waiting for since 1995. A girl recently told me she had brought her dog to a veterinarian school in Massachusetts to be checked out due to the fact that he had gone through several training classes to no avail. Their diagnosis, to our surprise, was A.D.D. She doesn't want to give him any medicine due to adverse side effects. He doesn't obey her and has no attention span. He can't LEARN to obey commands and runs all over in places he shouldn't be. I asked her, "How about giving him herbs?"

She replied, "He's OK. I love him the way he is."

I thought, "Wow, no-one ever said that to me. My mother DID pray for me, and for that I'm grateful."

Back to 1995 writings: *When* I went to school, all I did was look out the window and daydream all day anyway. *Are we having* FUN *yet*? It's poor judgment on the part of the school department which allows the inconsistency of teachers who aren't equipped to teach children in between retarded and intelligent. GOD HELP US ALL! These are the children running our country today. Stop the world, *I want to get off!* But there *is* hope.

The "60's" started a group of wonderful people who *cared* and finally *showed it* and *did something* about it. Where are you today?

In a life where our parents said, "*Keep your mouths shut* and don't tell anyone *anything* about you or us. Go about your own business, you'll stay out of trouble that way." Stay *within the lines* like in kindergarten. Well, DON'T STAY *within the lines* anymore. Get out from behind the curtains, THAT'*S why we're in trouble today.* Don't leave it up to your neighbor. If everyone did *ONE good deed* a day to keep this sad world from dying, even anonymously, we would *all heal* much faster and there would *finally* be hope where there was none.

Do what I do and my mother did before me. I *used* to be embarrassed as a child when she approached people. I didn't know she was healing everyone she came in contact with at the time. Look into people's faces, see what they need and then *give it*! I hear people yelling at their children in the stores. I seek them out like a heat bomb. I smile at the child. Whatever is needed, I do and say. Never has anyone *ever* said to me, "Mind your own business." I do it with God's love and you will too. If these people are *this abusive* to children in a *public area* (which is *a cry for* HELP), what are they doing behind closed doors? I had a lot of verbal abuse growing up. *I don't want it around me* ANYWHERE, ANYMORE!

Example: One father in a store was saying to his little boy, who was about five years old, "Jump out of the shopping cart." He didn't tell him how to do it. The child had no room to do so, and the mother just looked on. SHE *didn't speak up.* SHE *wasn't protecting her own son.* The father asked, "What are you a girl?" My first thought was, "What's wrong with being a girl?" No wonder children are killing and abusing animals and other children. Wake up parents! It's really happening and guess what, it *really is* YOUR *child.* So I said to this person, "He'll be thinking of you when he's forty years old and seeing a shrink."

The father replied, "I'm fifty-five and seeing one."

I thought, "You know, we really *are* what we eat, aren't we?"

You can only teach your children what *you* learned from childhood, unless you seek out knowledge and learn as an adult *another way, a better way, that's* what your children are going to be. Sad but true. If *you* don't tell them, *they* will need to seek out knowledge from others around them, as will your grandchildren and so it goes. To our future mass murderers and Jeffrey Dahmers, the children and adults that are abusing and killing animals: Get help! Go to a spiritual church and holistic healers if *your* church is not helping you. Try a hypnotist. That helped me with my depression and circles. I strongly suggest you go to someone with whom you feel safe and comfortable, who is trustworthy and good at regressing people to their past lives. I had it done and it was amazing. People have been cured of many things with much faster success than a psychiatrist such as fear of heights, water, relationships, cats, bugs, bulimia (which was popular hundreds of years ago) and so on. It works. Don't knock it until you've tried it. If that doesn't help get an exorcism. Satan (or an unhappy evil soul such as Hitler) has obviously taken them over, or they are *trying* to take them over, as they do with people who are now schizophrenic, anorexic, bulimic, alcoholic, etc., who admittedly say they feel like they have a demon around them. Who else would tell them to starve themselves, vomit, drink excessively or strike out at themselves or others. GET HELP!!!

One Sunday at a Spiritualist church, a girl who is schizophrenic approached me before service and looking everywhere but my eyes, asked if she could come to my home for a healing. I was shocked because in all the years I had seen her there she barely said, "Hi," to me or anyone else. I quickly took her to a private room and did a quick spirit cleansing on her, telling her to denounce and send away whatever spirits were attached to her space and aura and in fact running and ruining her life.

During the service I glanced at her. She was intently staring at the speaker. She seemed lighter and looked more aware. Afterward, she looked directly in my eyes and thanked me. Even her voice had changed and become stronger. She went on to tell me that for the first time in her whole life she clearly saw, heard and understood the service. At tea downstairs I noticed that within an hour her face looked once again lost and had a heavy dark tone to it. As I approached her, she quickly glanced down at the floor.

I asked her, "Did you let them back in?"

She said, "Yes, I got lonely and asked them where they went."

I asked, "Do you realize you open the door and invited them back in?"

Without making eye contact with me, she said, "Yes."

I replied, "I can do no more for you."

She said, "I understand."

Remember St. Michael said: "There are *evil spirits and Satan* wandering through OUR world trying to *ruin* OUR SOULS."

God: "YOU *are responsible for* YOUR *children*!

Teach these things in school."

Donna: "If your children, or others, are having nightmares that are staying with them, *scaring* them and waking them up, get them help. Don't wait until it's too late. In Egypt they say dreams *are OUR* REALITIES! Call to Archangel Michael for help to throw evil souls and Satan into hell and out of us once and for all. No, most of the time you can't feel spirits (evil or otherwise) come into you or leave you and it can happen over and over again. So BE AWARE!"

God & Donna: "*Don't close the door on* THAT! *Look* and *listen* for *their cry for help*. Especially if you notice that they're hurting animals or pushing kids and being the bully. Where do they *learn* this stuff? You'll pay for it one way or the other. It's against the law to kill animals. See how fast it gets rectified when the *parent* has to *go to jail with their children* for THEIR crimes. That will be a *real wake-up call for everyone*. If you see anyone abusing children or animals, call the Massachusetts Society for the Prevention of Cruelty to Animals, or whatever organization is in your state, then make *them* go out. Let's start an organization that will come out whenever we call them. One City is smart and caring enough to have a sensitive group of people who go into back yards and see if there are stray cats or any animals who need *humane* help. *For children call Social Services and make them go out.* Don't give your name if you don't want to, that's okay, and if you have to call again - do it!"

Donna: "On the other side of the coin, I was in a store one day and overheard a grandmother with her little granddaughter, who was fussing in the shopping cart about what she wanted *to eat* or *not eat*.

Finally the grandmother got upset and asked, 'What do you think life is, an OPEN *box of cookies*?' What a lesson! If I only knew *then what I know now*. If I saw how tough it was going to be all my life, I would not have wanted to be born. If I can lighten up, mix more cookies into my life, take it a minute at a time and smile more, especially at grouchy people, it would make life so much easier for me and others.

I just took the plastic off my lamp shades, they're over a year old. It's a freeing feeling, I guess I'm going to stay a while. Try it. Guess what? If they get dirty, you have an excuse to give them to a yard sale and donate the proceeds to the Humane Society, or give them to a charitable organization, and buy new ones, *brighter* ones. 'SMILE, *have a cookie!*' "

Chapter 7

Love Lite, Love Life

I'm around eight years old still living in the city, except instead of being on Norwell Street, I am now on Claybourne Street (as mentioned before), still in North Dorchester bordering Roxbury and within walking distance from Mother's Rest Park, Sportsman's Bar, the A & P Food Store, YMCA and a few miles from Codman Square. It was a long, cold walk to my new church, St.Peter's.

My niece, Elizabeth, was born on Elvis Presley's birthday (I have a brother who looked like a young Elvis), and was two years old when she died, while I was living on this street. It devastated me. She had leukemia. I remember seeing her arms purple from all the needles the doctors had put into her, trying to keep her alive while they searched for a cure. She suffered too much, yet even during her suffering, her beautiful eyes and smile would light up the room. In that very short time (for us, not her), she changed many lives and contributed a great deal of life's knowledge to everyone who met her, and through this book, those who have never met her.

God: " 'Sometimes you can't see it until the dust settles. But it's all there, you just have to look for it.' She is an *angel* now and she was an *angel* then. 'Unfortunately, sometimes parents' life problems come through their children.' She CAME to *leave and help*.

When you walk through a storm, hold your head up high."

Donna: "Even when I was *about* four years old, that song would always bring a tear to my eye?!"

February 22, 1999: Carol, one of my typists, will be THRILLED to type this. I'm having a lot more channeled to me for the whole book, but especially this chapter. I've come to the conclusion that there will always be a story to write about, so I'll have to save this other information for "*Book Two*" or I'll never get THIS book into the bookstores. It's also too soon to put into print some of the strange events, which have happened to me.

***

School was *more hurtful* at this time of my life, people told me to *study harder*. I would read the same page over and over, yet it wouldn't sink in.

"You can do better. You're lazy."

Probably, but it still won't sink in and when it does, it doesn't stay very long.

Wow, what a trauma. Talk about being closed in and claustrophobic. Oh no, NO, I CAN'T *do it*. What do you want from me? *You're* stupid! More walls going up. *Leave me alone*! *I* want to be alone! I NEED *to be alone*.

"She doesn't want to study. She COULD do it if *she wanted to.*"

HELLO, *I'm* HERE listening. *Hello*, who are the stupid ones? You are, if you are doing this to your siblings and friends or *whoever*. How can I go through life not knowing the simple things other kids and people know such as math, history, etc. The *fear* and *anticipation of confusing and humiliating failure*, after flunking so often, didn't help either. I still fight it off today. Some of the symptoms of A.D.D. are being impulsive, overactive, easily distracted, having a learning disorder and/or mild mental retardation.

Today, to reduce feelings of guilt in families, physicians tell them it isn't their fault. To improve the self-esteem of the children, physicians encourage the children to channel their energies into other activities to keep themselves busy and focused. When untreated in childhood, the child often has a negative attitude toward school and patterns of failure in his life. Three to seven percent of the school population have symptoms of A.D.D., which is usually found more frequently in boys and is usually noticed before age five. I wish we had known this much about A.D.D. when I was a child.

My mother's prayers and now mine.

God: "*Listen to me now*."

Donna Marie: "Is it all in me somewhere?"

God: "No."

Donna Marie: "Then what?"

God: "I have to tell you something."

Donna Marie: "What?"

God: "You knew all along. Some day something would happen to help you to learn."

Donna Marie: "What?" (That did feel right.)

God: "I'm going to tell you."

(Then nothing comes. There's more space and more space and nothing is coming.)

Donna Marie: "*In* THIS *lifetime*???"

God: "You are like a flower on a tree, blooming with joy, life, happiness."

Donna Marie: "What's that symbolic of? Flower on a tree?"

God: "Life, *Life*, LIFE!"

Donna Marie: "Thank you!"

Seven days of hardly any sleep. I NEED MY SLEEP. I did sleep a couple of hours last night though.

God: "This is the way to open the door. A tree to heaven."

Donna Marie: "What has happened is the left side of my brain, the thinking part of the brain, the lawyer part, the accountant part has totally gone and allowed the right side of my brain, the sensitive part, the artistic part, the poet, the writer, and the spiritual part, to take over completely. Then, 'to no brain thought' at all, *just the soul*, I'm trusting and learning completely from God. There's no room for *me* to *think*."

Donna Marie still: "What is *it*?" This following sentence came in like a stereo, from the left, then to the right side of my brain. Then it finally entered the center of my head. *So* IT *is one*. (As follows:)

God: "Lite and love, life and love."

Donna Marie: "So it is one and the same?"

God: "Yes. Love over lite. Love over life until they are one."

Donna Marie: "I feel ecstasy right now. I'm going under as if in a very deep, deep meditation. Thank you." (2/99: I don't know why it's spelled "lite?" Everyone who types or edits tries to change it to "light.")

God: "Left of brain, thinking. Go away until you are ready to listen to someone *other than yourself.* My brain is stubborn ego. If you *think* you know as much, *why ask me*? Why read again more books, buying more tapes and then you do more shopping, more drinking, more gambling. Hide in FEAR *behind them.* Animals RUN *from pain* and so do people. 'Let go, let God.' Trust, prayer, meditate, fill that hole that is within you, your soul. Embrace your children. Just when you *thought* you knew it all. Your eyes *are* your soul. You will see whoever *you admire most*."

Chapter 8

1-4-3, I Love You

Donna Marie: "As I was growing up, I hated the color red. Why?"

God: "I don't like *you*."

Donna Marie: "What's *that* mean?"

God: "You have a familiar lifestyle. Your family wore brown colors, etc. *I don't love myself.* Chakra colors are in your body starting from the bottom up to your head, red, orange, yellow, green, blue, indigo, lilac, white all around you and pink for love. There's more you could learn about these. These colors are bright and loving, warm and happy. *That's* who you are now. Not dull afraid, hiding behind dark colors that say, 'I don't like myself. Hide!' Bright enough colors that say, 'I like myself, here I am, look at me, in the way that I love myself, see me.' Not to be confused with someone who's looking for love in all the wrong places. No tight clothes, forget it now. I don't like that it represents *hate against yourself*, lack of respect. Sad, sad, sad. Again, learn now to love yourself and get balance in your life. Get rid of the black and white. Find and embrace the grey in your life, *finally*."

Donna Marie: "Thank you 1-4-3, I love you."

God: "And you love yourself."

God to everyone: "Your angels are watching over you to guide and protect you. Speak to your good angels for help because the devil is there waiting for you to do something wrong, to allow him into *you*. *Don't let him in*!!! You *think* he will protect you? This is a contradiction in terms. He will *not* and you will pay dearly for it. For you will suffer in the final end. You should be protecting yourself from him, not letting him in or calling to him. *Don't do it*! It is *wrong*! Satan is the best kept secret so that he can get away with more. *God's light WILL protect you more*. Trust me and PRAY, pray like you have never prayed before. *Love*."

Donna Marie: "Wow!"

Chapter 9

We Are All One

A few months ago I prayed to Mother Mary to come to Massachusetts for a change. Places like Brockton or Roxbury which really need our prayers. On Tuesday, June 13, 1995, I could not figure out why I was so tired but I still dragged myself to a philosophy class which I had been attending for a few months. We sit in a circle and pray and also give messages, which are channeled, to one another. This night I received a message from an Irish woman. She said, "I see a very old woman hunched over, with a lot of wrinkles in her face around you. She is saying watch out for your bones and osteoporosis." I had been bent over in my chair all night not knowing why. I tried to sit up straight several times. Also my bones had been bothering me for quite a while.

Doctors said to me, "It's your age, we all have it when we get older." Then let THEM *go see a doctor. Don't get me started on doctors.....and I'm NOT THAT old. A day late and a dollar short (why didn't I think of that when I was with him?).* I would never discourage you from going to see one, but if you find no relief from them, try to find other alternative, complementary methods. If you don't start feeling better after three visits, go elsewhere *even* if they *claim* to be holistic. If something they say or do doesn't seem right, just don't do it!

After the message about my bones, I went to the health food store and bought vitamins to strengthen them, along with using my weights I feel much better now. I learned much later that I had a very serious calcium deficiency. Also my mother and two sisters have/or had problems with osteoporosis.

Getting back to the story: Since Tuesday, I had been going into *very deep* meditations, one minute sitting watching TV, the next, lying down almost completely *out of it.* On Wednesday, June 14, 1995, the news came on, I seldom watch it, but Mother Teresa was on. She's going to Fall River, which is South of Brockton and then to Dorchester, which is next to

Roxbury. I was so connected to her and she needed *so much* energy that I was totally drained. I could see her pain in her face and in the way she was *hunched over*. There *is* a universal mind. I could feel where she was every moment that she was in Boston. We all love you and need you in our lives, Mother Teresa.

God: "Her work is almost done here. She will finish her/God's tour, go home, finish a lot of business there, then lay to rest."

Donna: "God bless her sore bones and wrinkled face of others sorrows. I will pray for her when she is going to the other side."

A couple of days later, I spoke to the Irish woman who had given me the message in class and told her of my experience.

She immediately got the chills and said, "I am honored that Mother Teresa would come through you *to me*. After all, who am I?"

God: "*We* ARE *all one.*"

Donna: "Thanks, Mother Teresa, for warning me about my sore bones and for coming to us in our hour of need. And thanks Mother Mary, for answering my prayers through Mother Teresa. I love you. Please protect us."

Saturday, August 24, 1996: The Boston Herald; "Doctors say that Mother Teresa's condition is deteriorating. Doctors put her on a respirator Thursday when her heart stopped beating for nearly one minute. She was revived with electric shocks. Mother Teresa, a Nobel prize winner, has maintained a grueling pace at her missions and orphanages in India and abroad, despite failing health." (I feel she was *revived* by God.)

God: "Hold on Mother. You're job is not yet done."

Mid morning I saw her face before me on TV and then I heard God say softly but clearly to her, "It's time. You can go now." That made her very happy, Mother Teresa was ready.

I heard just a few hours later that Mother (Saint) Teresa, had moved on into God's light of life.

The Patriot Ledger: Friday, September 12, 1997:
Powerful, poor, gather for funeral.

She and Princess Di are on the same road to heaven after graduating from the same school: *College of Real Life Experiences*. They will be in the same church over there, except Mother Teresa will be on the altar and Princess Diana will be in a front pew. God will come to them and say, "Tell me about your experiences and what you have learned."
"Only through silence, can the *truth* be heard," Mother Teresa.
I love you and I'll miss you.

***

Nostradamus predicted your father's fate, and he also said that July of 1999, would bring some bad things.
Goodbye for now to JFK Jr., your wife Carolyn and her sister Lauren Bessette. - July 1999

Chapter 10

Messages From God

Pray for your children and everyone. The worse they are, the more you send them *the white light of God*. The more angry you want to be at them, the more *light* you send them and of course the more angry you get, the more you hurt yourself, so let it go and *white light* yourself. You will see a difference in them *and you* but at some point they must also pray for themselves! If deep down in their soul they want to change, you will help them to change and they will help themselves to change for the better.

"Some people are like owls. The more light you shine in their eyes, the less they see," said Satan.

One time a young girl came into my home and said, "This feels different, calmer or something. How do I get my home to feel this way?"

How to White Light Yourself, Your Home and Others

God: "Take a few minutes, sit privately, get comfortable, don't cross your legs and arms. Take at least three very deep cleansing breaths in through your nose down deep into your system, hold it for six seconds and slowly release the negativity out through your mouth, do this *whenever* you need to. Now RELAX and meditate on what your needs are, but first pray that you're a better person. After your little meditation and prayer, and now being totally relaxed, bring the bright white light through your head and all the way down through your body. Just *relax* and picture it flowing through your head, heart/soul, arms, stomach, legs, and feet, then down through your toes pushing all negativity out of your fingers tips and toes visualizing it going up to the sky, past the clouds until it's out of sight. Now come back and feel, see and sense all the radiating light vibrating in and around you. Then mentally push all this beautiful spiritual white love light of peace through your fingers into all of the rooms, till it is forced out of all the doors and windows of wherever you are, now mentally picture anyone else's home, car, etc., and send your loving light there and then around our world, we should do this collectively to heal the world. Then think of the person or animal you would like to bless with *God's white light,* this *love light, life light.* Think of them, picture them and then bring white light through their head and down through their souls and hearts, continuing down through them until it comes out of their feet and hands, paws and all around them to protect them also. Peace will come to you and yours. You will see a difference. When you're at peace, your home will also be at peace. Your children, your pets and your plants will also be at peace. Feel the difference when you walk in your front door. The tension that used to be there will be replaced by calmness. *God does* come through trees, plants, animals, *all* people and children. When you get in touch with *that,* you are THERE. Unconditional love for yourself, everyone and everything, including the animals, here in this universe. *Say a prayer.*"

Chapter 11

A Chosen Person

God: "Say a prayer for enlightenment and you will become awake. And *you will become awake– do it now*! Go to the light before the love light goes out altogether. Please do not wait for emergencies and disasters to bring out the love for the stranger next to you. Remember we are *all* sisters and brothers and color blind. Every single job *is* important, but do it with love. Every single thought of love and act of love is noticed. *We see it all, we know it all.* When you are alone, you are *not* alone. Don't do it. Don't live a life of sin and *think* you are alone. *We see all, we know all.*"

Donna Marie: "Who is *we*?"

God: "God and his fellow helpers."

Donna: "Who are???"

Helpers: "*We* are the numbers of people that have gone before."

Donna: "What are your names?"

Helpers: "Our names are the people *you* NEED at the time."

At the SAME TIME that message came to me, a name of someone came to me whom I was to meet the following day, it's an unusual name which I had been trying all day to remember. This seemed very strange even for me and even more awakening. Sometimes you take for granted what's happening to you. I let go of my thinking process so much now (my left side of my brain) and put my heart and soul totally in the hands of God. Every once in a while something I write even surprises me. I'll continue.

Donna: "God, who is with me now?"

God: "God."

Donna: "Anyone else?"

God: "No."

Donna: "Why do you say *fellow* helpers? Why not woman, too?"

God: "So that *you* can define *me* from *you*."

Donna: "What? Why not woman, also?"

God: "So we can copy the styles of the day to see *us as we are*."

Donna: "What? Clear please. Women are helpers, too?!"

God: "No, *they* are *learning* to help themselves to be better at *being themselves at home*."

Donna: "I don't understand?"

God: "You will some day."

Donna: "When?"

God: "Now."

Donna: "OK? What? Please?"

God: "We are supposed to take care of everyone but ourselves, most *women think*. Women do *not* take care of themselves enough today. Their energy is on *everyone* and everything else on this side (earth). So as a result a lot of women do not have the freedom of coming back to help heal others on your plane, on a *higher* level."

Donna: "What can I tell powerful women on this plane regarding that?"

God: "They will be higher if they have *learned on your side, so they don't have to spend precious* time here learning, INSTEAD *of healing* on *your side*. Learn here, so you can heal here (on earth)."

Donna: "*Thank you*. I now understand. Could you tell me why you chose me?"

God: "You have an ability to sell your personality to others so *we* can come to you and tell you what to do to ease the pain of the world."

Donna: "Incredible! *Here we go again!* How do we do that?"

God: "Take all of your knowledge and bring it to the people."

Donna: "How?"

God: "Build *it* and they will come."

Donna: "I need a lot more than that."

God: "It is okay to sell people on an idea, but you can sell people on a belief of love and God. Don't go beyond your belief system, which *is going on forever*. To tell people and show people love, go beyond yourself and I will be there."

Donna: "I like that, thank you. People are going to think you should have come to someone with 150 IQ and wealthy."

God: "You were born into *this*. You shall bring my word *now*!"

Donna: "What if I didn't?" (I asked this question with respect, but remember, even my questions were channeled to me.)

God: "You will not survive."

Donna: "What does *that* mean?"

God: "Die and go where you learn to obey from the beginning of time."

Donna: "What beginning of time?"

God: "At the beginning of time we start at the beginning. Adam and Eve's mistakes, doing things over and over until we get things right. Do them *right* now or else we go back in time to do it again, to the other side."

Donna: "People might think I'm going crazy."

God: "That's beside the point. (People) *DON'T TEST ME*!!!"

Donna: " I won't, but please protect me."

God: "I will, but don't disappoint me."

Donna: "How can I if I am just letting you come through me?"

God: "You could not go to the people. *Only you* can decide that."

Donna: "Show me the way and I will go."

God: "Yes. Start by calling an agent about this writing even as we speak. Please tell the people we want to love them and protect them from all evil."

January 1999: I still can't figure out why I needed to call an agent in "1995," which I did to no avail, when we're still adding and editing in 1999. The small publisher I contacted who *claimed* to be *very* spiritual will not return my calls, or this book which then was entitled *My Talk With God*.

Chapter 12

What Legacy Are You Leaving Behind?

God: "Speak to me of your life and love with your children. Are they happy? Are they sad and lonely? Are they happy to be alive? I don't think so, otherwise why would they be killing themselves, others and animals? *You* brought them into this world, *now* YOU take care of them. Teach them, love them, worry about them, and where they are. Then realize YOU are responsible for what they *do* and *don't* do in this life. Please do not make excuses, '*not* MY child.' I wonder who is committing *all* of these crimes? It's the parents. If you go to jail for the children that are in your care you would realize, maybe I had better take some responsibility for this life that I am responsible for, this life I brought into the world. Stop passing the buck for *your* responsibilities. If they do something wrong, own up to it, don't try to sweep it under the rug or put it in a closet. Stop blaming the police."

Donna: "I saw a program where a white man turned in his son for starting fires. When police are looking for someone who has committed a crime, they start with children who have killed or abused animals, and children who have started fires."

God: "Get help for them now! Do us all a favor, whatever *it* takes, *do something*!"

Donna: "As I am typing this, a news report is interrupting a TV program: An attorney was just shot to death for prosecuting a gang member. A *nineteen*-year-old boy shot and killed him. (In 1999 the black gang member was just now picked up.) Also, a boy in his teens stole a bus one day. He literally ran over cars, people and police whom he had trapped in an alley. They had to shoot him in the leg to stop him. His mother was trying to sue *the police* saying they shot him because he was black."

God: "What has this world been getting away with? *Stop it, stop it now*! Don't blame the teachers either. Parents tie *everyone's* hands then *they* do not take responsibility for their children. Then they wonder, 'W*hy* me? Why him? Why her?

Why *my* children?' Some teachers are, unfortunately, being programmed to *bow down* to parents rather than stand up for what *is right. Could one reason be that some principals get a salary plus extra money for every child who stays in school? You all* are creating our present and future problems in this world. YOU *are responsible* FOR THAT! If you can't handle the children, give them to someone who can, even to the police if they have done wrong."

God & Donna: "This *is a sad* day for all of us. This is a very sad day for Martin Luther King who had a dream. Someday I hope our children will be able to walk down the street and be judged by their *good character* instead of the color of their skin. All of the negativity *you* put out comes back to *you.* All of the love you put out (in soft spoken language) *will come back to you. Pray for love of every color!* We *are* all related.

I have a dream ...someday *all* of *our* children will be able to walk down the streets *without being killed*! Take children of any nationality away from parents who are afraid to give them *boundaries.* Do not let peer pressure force you into having children if you don't feel you are meant to have them. There are plenty of people in their eighties who have no children and are content.

Discipline and firmness with love are necessary when raising children. When you make a rule *back it up, don't give in,* out of LOVE, or you're lost and everyone around you and that child is *lost* FOREVER. They will grow up, or not grow up, with that same negative belief system and *attitude.* They will end up with unrealistic ideas of what *life* is *really* about. As a result they will be incompetent in *this real world. Keep a firm hand* with them, but do not abuse them in any way or you will pay! If you are mentally or sexually abusing children, *stop it now* and *cleanse yourself, pray* for *yourself now* just by talking to *God. Don't wait*! Cleanse *now,* then pray for the children again and again until they heal. YOU have to heal yourself! Stop *your* circles *now*! Find a way to break the cycle. It is out there. Remember, you are their parent, *not* their friend. Are *you afraid* that if you show them authority you will lose them? You *will gain their respect.* Mothers and fathers, grandmothers and grandfathers, let go of your own ego, YOUR stubborn ego and teach these children *that when their lifestyle is* wrong, you're *not* going to *tolerate it*, and *the outside world is not going to tolerate it* ANYMORE!!! Are you leaving them with your love? Are you *showing* them how to be ambitious and how to have pride IN *themselves*?"

Donna: "There's a detective in Boston who showed city kids how to plant flowers around town. While on a bus ride, Jan, Samantha, and their daughter, Kristen, saw these kids smiling and talking. They really seemed to be enjoying what they were busy doing."

God: "If EVERYONE did that what a beautiful world this would be! It would have to be *everyone,* because some people are so lazy that if I said, 'every OTHER person', you would leave it up to the OTHER *person. You* KNOW *you would*!"

Donna and God: "'Show your children *good lessons.*' Are you showing them, *God forbid*, how to verbally and physically abuse people and animals which will eventually send them to a psychiatrist, jail and Hell? Everywhere I go it seems that parents are verbally abusing their children, calling them names such as 'stupid.' Many men call their sons 'girls' and mothers tell their daughters they are 'stupid'. Do you listen to yourselves? You *better*! Also, sperm and egg donors, please stop making children who will *never* know who their fathers and mothers are! People will be marrying their own brothers and sisters. When your children come home, look into their eyes and ask them, 'Did you make me proud of you today?'

There are people who come into the United States, who can't even speak English, yet they become millionaires within a couple of years. That's what America and living is all about, working hard, being fair, God-like, honest, happy *and going forward.* I would rather see people do *that* rather than stay on welfare. Using welfare in hard times is one thing, making it a career for yourself and your children is another. The state shouldn't allow that. Families using it *forever,* as a career, is a sin."

"Did *you* make *me* proud today?" *God*

Chapter 13

Our Dream

I have the same dream from God over and over again. We are in a very large stadium with thousands of people. Over a year ago I received a message that I would be healing over a thousand people at one time within two years.

God through Donna: "There will be spiritual healers in a circle around everyone with lights low. There will be meditating prayer, songs, laughing, crying, soul searching, healing stories, love and togetherness. It starts with arms around each other's shoulders, praying for others, children, animals, our planet and ourselves. We pray to God and have God in each and everyone of us. We *are* one *God*! Take your skins off, look into your neighbors' eyes/souls, what do you see? Aren't we all the same under our skins? Cleanse yourself, of *your own* cruelty, *your own* hate. Open up your own heart and soul."

You will see whoever you admire most.

Donna: "This just came to me: *I* can't help falling in love with *you*."

God: "And YOU with YOURSELF. There will also be contributions for the young children in the streets of the United States of America, the homeless cats and the bewildered."

Donna: "I would like to start in our own back yards first."

God: "*Then* go around the world."

Chapter 14

Live And Let Live

CONTROLLING PEOPLE: Someone owns the company you work for, *but that person doesn't own you.* Someone owns the apartment you live in, but that person doesn't own you. Sales people are *supposed* to be nice to you, not act arrogant towards you. When they get upset, no matter over what, I/we feel fear and try to over-compensate by being nice, THEN the vicious circle begins. I get hurt and used (sometimes) and angry. *I was* FORCED *as a* CHILD to stay in bad relationships of verbal abuse and controlling brothers and sisters. I was alone and confused. I had a difficult time standing up for myself trapped in an apartment with "control freaks" *when* they were home. I felt like a punching bag. My mother said some negative things when I was in my teens and into my early twenties. As a result her words programmed and confirmed my insecurities, of uselessness and not feeling pretty. Along with the confusion from her words of, no guy is good enough for me, OR I'm not good enough for THEM!? I learned it was out of fear from her life's experiences at those ages, saying to me, "I don't want you to go through what I did," but never telling me what she had experienced. No wonder I had claustrophobic feelings in marriage, breaking out in sweats - fight or flight; most of the time *flight.*

January 1999: P*sychiatrists are going to have a field day with this book. It may become mandatory reading in.... .... "Psych -101".*

God: *"Break through with love."*

Donna Marie: "What am *I* afraid of? THEY don't pay my rent!? Will I get thrown out on the street? Then what?"

God: "Get over *it.*"

Donna: "My fear CREATES *anger*. I feel my fear in my upper chest, heart, then in my throat; then I push it down to my stomach (my Achilles heel) and I make MYSELF sick."

God: "Sad, awful! Let go, let God."

Donna: "If something *is* wrong in work or the apartment or when I'm trying to buy something, why do *I* feel fear? I'm right; *they*'re wrong. I hear my sister say, '*The boss Is* NEVE*R wrong*'. (ha, ha). Same as childhood, the MAPS are of *then* and *now* OVER *one another*, same *stuff. The circle* STOPS *here and now*.

A good example involves a male acquaintance who just called me. After speaking to him, I had a feeling of *not* being good enough. Then I realized he *wanted* to instill that *in* me, because he felt that way about *himself.* He owes me peace of mind as a friend, and *I owe myself* peace of mind because I LOVE *myself.* God, please help me to *learn* how to handle *this* situation *now.*"

God: "Stick up for yourself."

Donna: "Not working, God. I still feel fight or flight. I feel SCARED. Fear gives me nausea. I yell and sometimes even swear."

God: "Talk to them. Express how you feel so you *don't yell or swear.*"

Donna: "Help me with fear of asking and communicating. *Cleanse my soul.* Oh, dear God, I am *trapped again.* STILL!!! In MYSELF! I feel something releasing, a little tingling down my back. I *am* a nice person. I like nice things. I am *sorry if that bothers you* (people). You have your own garbage. Let me live my life as I choose and get through *my* lessons. I have been good to you. Leave *me* alone! *Leave me alone!!*"

God: "Be careful not to live for other people."

Donna: "That's *it*! *How* wonderful, *safe*. Thank you, God. *Now* to keep this with me on a day-to-day basis."

God: "*Pray!* Live and let live as long as they are not killing anything or anyone. Do your own thing. Don't get caught up in other peoples' garbage. Be centered and go forward but more importantly be happy where you are. If someone around you keeps bringing you down, whether verbally or physically, get *rid of them.* Sometimes just ignoring them is *not enough.* Let people live to make their own mistakes. If that bothers *your* lifestyle, ***leave*** and live your own life, NOT THEIRS or ANYONE ELSE'S."

Donna: "Why is it that when I buy something on sale, bring it home and love it, I just *have* to have another one?"

God: "Because you don't like yourself."

Donna: "What does *that* have to do with it?"

God: "You *have* to like yourself in order to *stay in* yourself. Not to *hide* behind others and things like shopping, smoking, drinking, food or whatever. *Live for yourself!!!*"

Donna: "I liked the structure of the condominium I used to own by the water, which had security guards, tennis courts, a pool, etc., luxury, luxury, luxury, but it was very structured, intense and stay within the lines. It gave me a semblance of peace and the appearance of having *it* together. The place I moved to across the street, is a much smaller complex and has very little luxury, although it's a very nice apartment and I still have water views. One friendly neighbor at my new address said, 'We're not like that here, we're more relaxed.' "

"I don't feel *that* comfortable with this way of life. Am I too structured? Is it time for me to find the *grey* area? The maps of my life again. What lesson is in this?"

God: *"Roll with the punches,* EMBRACE *the grey, I love you!"*

Donna: "Thank you. *I love you too!*
What do I do to make ME happy?"

God: "*I* don't know!"

Donna: "Good one! The more *within* I go, the more I care about what *I* think about myself and who *I* am, NOT what everyone else thinks of me!"

Say your name and/or *whoever* else needs a prayer.
I, Donna Marie Howard,
Ask for a COMPLETE soul,
in the name of
the Father, the Son and the Holy Ghost!

Donna: "God, when I act like nothing is wrong, the energy around me changes. Let me leave with love and giving love, instead of stewing *in my pain."*

God: "Give *it* back to them all and then out to the universe. As *good* as you are, that is how *bad* you can be! Don't allow *anyone* to push *you* around. Push them back, then turn the other cheek and forgive them. Don't STAY in a position to be pushed again. God says lighten up, *have fun, stop being sad."*

Donna: "Thanks for giving me permission to let go. (I actually feel that negative energy leaving my arms, especially my right arm.) There has to be a grey area, one part of my life too structured, the other not structured enough. So I have to balance *it* and keep *it in* BALANCE!!! "

God: *"Fearless, peaceful, and never alone. This* IS *my Bible*!!!

I have a way of stripping people down to the bone marrow; a stillness comes over them; *they* work on *themselves* and now begins the healing process. And heal!

I'll abuse you so much

YOU'LL HEAL!!!

For every time there IS a reason, a time for
EVERY PURPOSE

UNDER THE SUN!"

Chapter 15

Mary's Mother

Donna: "No one mentions *MARY'S MOTHER*???"

I just got a little release feeling like trickles of water up my back then down the back of my arms, and at the exact same time
I saw a vision of my mother.

She is still alive.

Is it just symbolic?

God: "Yes, because she is

your mother of POWER *and* LIGHT,

as was Mary's MOTHER!"

Chapter 16

Music *IS* Healing God's Thoughts

Donna: "I have to depend on spirit and God because of my Attention Deficit Disorder. I have a hard time reading and as a result I read very little."

God: "Don't be *too sensitive* to people's writings. The *well* is *never dry*. Leave here because *your lessons are done, not* out of *fear*!"

Donna: "Wow, what wonderful messages. I am *very* tired now, *please* pull back and give me the strength I need to do what you *so delicately* are steering me to right now.

So much for *that*! Well I need these lessons anyway. Thank you."

From God: *"I'LL be with you forever! Listen to the words of 'That's* what friends are for.' "

Donna: "I needed that message, thank you. Songs are what *I* can relate to from day to day in real life! When I hear them on the radio, they *do* remind me of God. I believe God and his helpers give poets, song writers, and many authors, such as Dickens, their words. If you stop long enough and listen, these feelings and words will come to you also. Remember something very important: What you bring to the party is a reflection of how you feel about the people around you. If you have a lot of money and bring little or nothing, it shows the people around you how you feel about them and you've missed out on the great feeling of TRUE giving and love. If you have little money, let people know ahead of time, so as not to be embarrassed. True friends will still make you feel welcome, wanted, comfortable and loved regardless of your circumstances. Your friends should lovingly teach you about reciprocating if your family and friends have not done so before. On the other hand, people with money, who are intentionally like Scrooge, won't be as lucky as he was in the end. How many of us have been open enough to see our past, present and future, especially our own wakes? For example, how many people show up and how do they feel about us, the way Scrooge learned from looking into his future with his angel of death. Ahhh, Dickens, I love you ... you WERE, and ARE so *there*!!! Thank you so much for bringing God's works to us."

God: "That's why you and others are very nice to people at the beginning ... high expectations."

Donna: "What exactly does *that* mean?"

God: "People want what they can't have. Be with someone out of LOVE."

Donna: "Can I finish these thoughts, please? I've had a hard time finishing things all my life. 'Teacher, teacher,' came to me."

Donna: "*This is* my temple."

God: "*Wherever you are,* IS your temple. Tell me what you see at night while you're sleeping. IS IT ME? I vow to be one with all of you. *I look into your eyes and I see*, there's *nothing that can take your love away from me for eternity.*"

Donna: "Beautiful, thank you! I feel it's similar to Hercules, half human and half God. His mother was of earth and his father from above."

God: "*You* are responsible for *you*. The hero *is* you!!! YOU!!!"

Samantha and Carol said that when they're singing certain hymns and their choir is in perfect harmony and balance, they feel joyous or almost tearful at times at the beauty and blend of the words and music. Finally, a wonderful feeling of peace, cleansing, and wholeness comes over them.

As the old saying goes, "Those who sing pray twice."

Chapter 17

The Dead Shall Walk Amongst Us: The Cape

The summer of 1995:

A few days have passed. The ants are gone now that I am going to the Cape. I am all packed and there is some pounding in the attic that I haven't heard since Dennis left. Maybe the spirits up there are saying good-bye and have fun *or* don't come back. But as I said before, that's another book. That's why I'm happy to be bringing my cat Bartet, so *they* won't bother her here. As it turned out, I would have been very lonely without her.

I keep getting the name "Mary" in my head and cannot get rid of it.

William, the best landlord I've ever known, is on his way here to put some ant powder by the sliding door. ("1999": As it turned out we NEVER needed it, and I didn't like it in the house anyway.) Then I'm going to follow him back to his home on the Cape which he has put on the market to sell. We arrived there a short time later after having a pleasant ride, except the name Mary was still ringing in my head. Before me was this absolutely gorgeous home on a dead-end street abutting twenty five acres of conservation land surrounded by powerful, strong, tall oak trees.

As I walked through the front door I could feel a peace come over me. I looked down at the sunken living room and up at one of the three very tall cathedral ceilings in awe. It takes a lot to impress me because I had seen a lot of beautiful homes while I was in the real estate business for over fifteen years. I could not believe it had not sold yet and wondered why. Maybe some ghosts didn't want anyone to live here, or for the house to sell. My true feeling is that William doesn't *really* want to sell this beautiful house. It occurred to me that Bartet and I were going to be in this very large house for as long as we wanted, and yet, I still felt no fear.

Although it was furnished, he hadn't lived there for a long time, so there were a lot of daddy long leg spiders around. In spite of this the house appeared clean. My cat was thrilled about the spiders! I was not. I WAS grateful for her company. I asked William to turn the grandfather clock off, because it was a little too much like the Twilight Zone for me. Before he handed me the key and left for his other home, he showed me the loft. I felt distinctly uncomfortable up there. I knew I wasn't going to be alone after all. Later on, I discovered the name I had been thinking of at home and on the ride all the way down here was a *ghost* named Mary.

God knows who else is here.

After, I settled in to continue writing this book, ("No television" a little bit of an addiction but at least I watch more educational programs than before. I still enjoy comedies also.) I was getting a little bored, so I started calling people. I was talking to Sandy, a spiritual person I know, and asked her if she felt anyone with me (as I had) and what the name might be. She *thought* a minute then said, "Margaret."

I said, "You *know* it's Mary. Why did you say Margaret?" She said, "*I thought* Mary seemed too simple when it came to me. See what happens when *you think* instead of listening to *your soul*. *You* change things that should *not* be changed."

I said, "Tomorrow, when I'm not so tired, I will pray for Mary to go to heaven, to the *white light*."

I was telling Sandy that I'm burning cedar incense to "cleanse" the house, and as I said that, I noticed it had gone out in the middle. I went over to the incense and told Sandy, "there's a large drop of water that put it out." Looking all around I said, "Where did that come from?"

Sandy said, "It's a tear drop." She felt the same chills as I had before, going up her back and down the back side of her arms. So much for the "cleansing the house of spirits *with cedar*" theory!

"Well, Sandy, it looks like *it* can't wait until tomorrow." I felt a great deal of loneliness, confusion and sadness from Mary. I felt it would obviously be better to send her to God's light now. I asked Sandy to help me pray for Mary. I called for someone from the other side to help, especially St. Michael for protection. I could see Mary walk to the light, to her mother's waiting arms. They embraced at the threshold then Mary said to me, "Thank you, I love you, *be happy.*" She's in God's light now where she belongs, not in this house which was limbo for her. I felt again like I was at a funeral, but what replaced Mary's sadness, confusion and loneliness was now lifting off of me and was replaced with peace, happiness and love. Also, thanks, Sandy, for your assistance.

Well, it's 11 P.M., which is the time I used to go to bed when I was able to sleep. I'll give it a try. I was tossing and turning, while my cat was *under* the bed, which was *very* disconcerting because she normally slept on a chair or under a blanket on the bed. Midnight, the clock radio next to the bed went on, not a minute before, not a minute after. Now I'm lying here listening to the music thinking - it's pretty obvious there is *another* spirit here. I turned it off and angrily said, "Leave me alone! I came down here to get some sleep. I'm exhausted." I got up, turned on a night light, the stereo and got to sleep around 7 A.M.

The real estate lady woke me up at 8 A.M. I was not crazy about her waking me up that early just to tell me she MIGHT come by while I'm staying here. You never do that in business unless it's an emergency. Maybe *something* made her call to wake me.

A friend had suggested a real estate agent who was tops on the Cape, so I called her. She's going to stop down here in a few hours. In the interim I called William and asked him if he knew a Mary.

His reply was, "No...why?"

I then told him the story. I also asked if there was a dog living here before, because I could smell one around the bed. I told him my cat spent most of the night and part of the day under the bed. (Bartet is so cute. She just came into the room with cobwebs all over her whiskers. I had to stop writing to clean her up.) My sensitive landlord said, "I *do* believe in *this.* I buried my German shepherd in the backyard, and *I* do feel him around me when I come to visit the house."

No wonder Bartet was *under* the bed and I felt so safe and protected in such a large, unfamiliar home. And *no, William* did not set the alarm clock for midnight as a joke. Anyway, I knew he wouldn't do that.

I was going to water his plants, and while looking in the cupboard for a large glass, a beautiful handmade mug kept drawing me to it. I picked it up, and Someone kept saying, "Turn it over, turn the mug over." When I did, I was stopped dead in my tracks. Engraved on the bottom was the name Mary. Tears came to my eyes. I was *overwhelmed*.

The broker I had called stopped by. I liked her much more than the sales person who woke me so early. She had the sensitivity to match people up to homes with love, as I used to do, rather than just *sell* to get money. We were talking about spiritualism, so I told her about Mary and showed her the mug. It touched her soul as it had mine. William said he would give the real estate lady a call, and was surprised to hear about Mary's name being on a mug, yet he still had no clue as to who Mary was.

If people don't pay for healing, they just don't listen. I ran out to get Bartet and me some lunch. I was influenced to go to the Chinese restaurant (always listen to your inner voice UNLESS it tells you to do something wrong). I met a young woman who had a *triple bypass*. Her father died at a very young age from a *heart attack*. Please *do not* let your family's illnesses influence your mode of death.

God: "We *have been* preprogrammed, but let's change that old movie *now*!"

Donna: "I told her to go out and sing and dance more. She said, "I love to dance, but I haven't done that in *years'*."

God: "Don't we create our own happiness or sickness."

When I returned with our lunches, Bartet and I took a couple of minutes to sit out on the beautiful, large balcony. The wind picked up a little. The oak trees started bowing deeper and deeper. We *are all connected*, we *are all* connected, EVERYTHING *and* EVERYONE!

God: "You have a lot to learn."

Donna: "Still?" (Oh, brother).

God: *"Unconditional love."*

Donna: "Large black ants started to parade up onto the balcony so I figured it was time to go in and write again."

8:30 P.M.: I was speaking to a friend again on the phone. *Now no TV is driving me nuts!* I feel like I'm on a sabbatical.

God: "How deep is your love?!! You're living in a world of evil people trying to destroy you. I'm your *light* in your deepest, darkest hour."

Donna: "Thank you, God. I get the point."

The next day I went home. I couldn't sleep in William's beautiful home either, and I had learned the lessons I needed to know. So it was time to go.

Shortly after that I spoke to William. He said he had taken the house off of the market, and was now living in it and loving it. He said, "You cleansed it for me, getting rid of the negativity, making it possible for me to move back in! It feels good here now, I'm happy to be home and I'm no longer allergic to cats. You did a good job. Thank you."

The only problem with *that* is, he *was* going to let me use his house again with my friends in the future. It seems every time my ship comes in I'm at the airport!

Anyway, I'm glad I could help him. He's a great guy and a wonderful landlord. William is a handsome man inside and out, and more intuitive than he realizes. I know there is a connection between us from THE PAST. He was very understanding of me when I hurt my stomach and back on the job. I don't know where I'd be, or what I would have done without his support, he has no idea 'til he reads this paragraph how much he has enabled me to write this book and others. Thank you William from the bottom of my heart.

Sandy and I must have cleansed his house spiritually more than we realized. He now has a wonderful, sensitive, new, pretty girlfriend, whom I really like.

God: "Yes, he started anew."

Chapter 18

Relationship Circles

Sandy started the phone conversation by saying, "*I have to* tell you something." (*Lessons for me.*) The old feelings of "Oh, oh, what did I do?" Even though *I knew I* did nothing wrong. What *is that*? I did things and lied as a child to cover up, but *I was surrounded by Indians. Sad feelings* and *no feelings*! Who's sorry now?

Sandy and I were *supposed* to go to Bill's house to buy some healing herbs. Bill had recently spoken about the herbs at one of our philosophy classes. She and I agreed later that when we first met him we did not think one way or the other about him. No attraction *at all*. But during the class, every time I thought something, he seemed to bring it up. At one point I had asked him if he was psychic. He just smiled. But I felt that he and I were connected somehow.

By the end of the class, Sandy and I both thought he was *wonderful*. Don't ask me why or how! She mentioned later she hadn't had feelings like that in a very long time. I haven't met anyone I liked in a long time either and neither one of us understood, "Why him?"

Sandy called me two days before we were supposed to go to his house to give me a lot of reasons why she had to go to his house alone. (None of which were true.) You didn't have to be psychic to figure out what was going on. I thought, "She saw how attentive he was to me in class, but if he wants her now, that's OK too." I could always tell when one of my *friends* was starting to like a man I was interested in or dating, as I'm sure most of you can.

God: "Everyone knows what you are thinking. NOWHERE TO RUN AND NO PLACE TO HIDE!"

Donna Marie: "When I was younger, I would say something to the girls about them flirting with my dates, then I'd still hang out with them, but just ignore them. When I was older, I wouldn't hang around with that type of a jealous girl who tries to steal your happiness, and if they get him they're *still* not happy! It would be one thing if they were 'meant to be' together, but some do it just because he's with you. There's the black and white showing up again. Where is my *GREY* area?"

God: "You are learning balance, but if it is someone who is *hateful*, you *do not* HAVE *to* stay around them."

Donna: "Were Sandy and I mirroring each other?" (Two people that are alike learning from one another.)

God: "No. *We* were seeing if you would learn your lesson. 'NO MORE CIRCLES.' "

Donna: "Sandy called to admit what I had already known. It must have been very hard for her. I was beginning to think she was competing with me or jealous. What's the story?"

God: "Be careful not to get someone out of your life from before, from whom you were supposed to learn *that lesson* about *yourself* and you didn't. Even if they weren't nice to you, they were there to *teach* you and *show* you your lesson. That's why you're here. While with a new or longtime friend, husband or wife, or those on your streets, and in your circles, who year after year still continually ask you why you said that, or treated them a certain way, learn about *your actions*, right or wrong, through *their* actions and words toward you. Listen to them, look at them, learn from your mistakes, then STOP THEM or else year after year someone *else* will remind you till the day you die! 'Why did you say or do that to me, why do you always go after someone else's man or woman?' 'That wasn't very nice of you.' 'Why do you drive so fast?' 'Why do you make fun of people?' I will mimic you and mirror you and your actions till you get IT and *finally* STOP IT. (Only the good die young.) That's why you are here, *to learn."*

"*Why* are *YOU here*?"

If Bill is for one of us, fine. If not, fine. If we need to learn a lesson from Bill and then move on, S*o Be It*! They're all *just* lessons. As it turned out, I went to Bill's house and swapped him a healing for some herbs.

As I was giving him a psychic healing, his mother came through loud and clear from spirit. It came to me, she was attracting every single woman around to her son, waiting on him hand and foot. I had been drinking a pot of coffee a day lately, as opposed to one cup of decaf. every few weeks or so. Bill said his mother drank a pot of coffee every day. She wanted him to get his house in order and settle down.

A woman was cleaning out his dishwasher when I arrived. His mother was breaking the law of God's universe by influencing women to wait on her son and by making them all want to date him. No one is supposed to influence any other person here or in the hereafter. And *I* don't want to be influenced now or ever by anyone. She was upset because he wasn't doing what *she* felt *he should* be doing with *his* life. She felt, and I agreed, that the dog she left behind was not being cared for properly. I helped him clean the dog's ears and suggested he give the dog a bath and take him to the veterinarian. I then said prayers to bless them all and let them go. But his mother wasn't going to let go that easily. She didn't feel my work, or hers, was done. The ball *was in his court* now.

I once saw a thick, clear, plastic shield come down in front of me when someone at the spiritualist church was about to give me a message. She stopped in mid-sentence, look at me bewildered, and walked away. I feel a mirror-like shield surrounds our earth and automatically reflects back on us all our good or bad actions.

I've learned a mother's prayers, emergency prayers and other prayers go directly to God, then filter down to people on earth so that we may help. If you don't help, you're not doing your angelic duty. He is watching you. At the same time, don't be used or become an en-abler. If you don't *share,* you're nothing. We all have God in us and around us. Unless you have brought evil into you, *then pray very hard to God and St. Michael to come to you or to send your earth angel to help you.*

There are different types of abuse, and ways of doing it. People who are too tired and too empty are having children and buying pets for all the wrong reasons, then neglecting them. There's no excuse for that. *Reach out* for help. *It's* all around you from here and up above. D*o not* abuse your children or pets.

Then there are the other types of hands-on abuse, where you are even more mentally ill. Neither type of abuse is right. It's not good enough to only give children a roof over their heads, is it? Pets and children need vets or doctors, love and care, food and baths. Just what *you* would have liked as a child.

***

Added in January 1999: Although I had cats all my life, no-one in my family ever brought any of them to a vet. Before Marco, we had never had names for the cats, except for, "The Cat." Now even my stray cats have names. In my late teens my friends educated me on taking care of my cats, and told me to take them to the vet's. As a result of their information, I took one of my animals, my beautiful Siamese cat Marco, for the first time to the vet's. My Mother softly confided in him every morning before anyone came downstairs for breakfast. Yet, when my mother heard what I was about to do, she howled, "Oh, my God, you're wasting good money!"

I said, "He's sick and needs his shots!"

She said, "No he's not. He'll be fine in a few days. There's nothing wrong with him."

I said, "Yes, there is. I'm paying and He's going."

She retorted, "There's something wrong with YOU!!"

When Marco came home and recovered within a few days, it taught and showed my mother something. I was never brought to a doctor, except for shots needed for school, not even when I chipped a bone in my ankle. The most I ever got was tomato soup (Irish "chicken" soup) when I was sick. If I was deathly ill I got an aspirin and a hot water bottle.

Samantha just asked, "You got a hot water bottle?" Ha-ha!

Just a note: Aspirin can be dangerous for children because it can cause Reyes Syndrome.

***

Back to Bill's mother: I could feel his mother's tears as I gave Bill the message about her dog. Because she was with me in spirit, the dog would not leave my side and attacked any of Bill's other pets who tried to come to me, even though he was only one third their size.

"If you're not going to take better care of my dog on this plane," she said, "have a vet humanely put him to sleep. Send my dog over to me. *I* will take better care of him. *I* love him."

I could feel her sorrow and tears more strongly now as *her* tears flowed through *my* eyes. It was a very sad thing for me as well because I love animals so much. She was not interested in making her son whole anymore. *She* was even more disgusted with him when she saw the full condition of her dog. I told her to go up for her lessons on the other side for bringing up such a child.

God: "We can help no more. We can only do so much. Why do *I* get blamed for everything *you create for yourself in this life* that has been *given to you in love*? You *are your own body and soul, create your own happy good life*. *You* all have a free will. If you didn't, we would all be perfect. You ALL DO have a free will, if you did not WE WOULD ALL BE PERFECT. I will pray for them from afar."

Donna: "His mother was controlling his life from the other side, *her needs*, not his."

God: "Who cares about *you* first? *You* for a change."

Donna: "My lesson: Twenty years ago, I dated a 'Bill' - only his name was Travis. They even looked alike, same height, same kind of vans, same stubbornness, same kind of controlling mothers, both Gemini's, only children, same groupies, same roommates with the *same names and personalities*. Both had animals. It then seemed every time I turned around in Bill's house, I saw Travis. Remember, I prayed for my negative circles to stop. If this was even two years ago, I would have gone out with Bill and made the exact same mistakes I made *twenty years* earlier. There are just no words to describe what this insight and lesson has meant to me, a map of my childhood over my adulthood. Different towns, different streets, same *stuff! I* can't even believe the similarities between Bill and Travis. I used to say to myself (knowing they were playboys), I'll just go out with them a couple of times and have some fun, a few dinners, some dancing. Lonely lies to myself! I passed this test!!! I never saw Bill/Travis again."

God: "Run as fast as you can and DON'T LOOK BACK. *Heal yourself*!!! HEAL YOURSELF!"

Donna: "We learn strange *things* at home, *don't we*."

God: "Yes."

Donna: "What is lacking *in them* to treat *us like that*?"

God: "It might be what they learned growing up, or *not* growing up!!! Or what they *didn't* learn."

Donna: "Like me suffocating my plant. God help us all! *Trust*!"

God: *"WE CAN DO NO MORE!"*

Chapter 19

We Will Overcome Now And Forever

Politics and religion: Let's talk a little about the Kennedys. Well, at least I know three of my books will sell. The Kennedys will borrow the book from Clinton, who *thinks* he's a Kennedy, or from one of *their* priests, (*God knows* what some of them *are thinking*) or perhaps a sale to a movie star!

3/99: I HAVE to say one more thing here! "Monica, Monica, Monica (one of President Clinton's former liaisons). Who do you think you are, Marilyn Monroe? It's all been done before. Did you know that you and Camilla, Princess Diana's husband's girlfriend, are mentioned in the Bible? There's a lot of unspoken embarrassment about our President and a lot of confusion about the First Lady's business dealings."

9/99: Clinton's office sent Monica's father a letter asking for money to help with Clinton's lawyer bills. The only problem with *that* is Clinton originally lied about having sex with Monica which also got her into trouble. Monica went to court and daddy has her bills to pay.

Also in 1999, U.S. Vice President Al Gore and *his friends* in the chemical *testing* industry are planning on killing "MILLIONS" of *innocent* animals! In his haste, GORE dismissed a crucial fact: most of these chemicals have *already* been tested. Many, like those in rat poison, are already KNOWN to be dangerous. Turpentine will be forced down animals throats and rubbed on their raw, injured skin, unless YOU call the following number: EPA Administrator, Carol M. Browner, Tel.:202-260-4700. *Demand* that it validate non-animal tests for use in the HPV chemical-testing program *immediately*. Call PETA for other *important* numbers. *Thank you*!! Gore always said he'd do *something* for the animals when he got *power*! Definition *of* GORE: BLOOD from a *wound*; to *pierce* with a *pointed instrument. Coincidence??*

Well, so much for OUR White House.

"Need I say more?"

God: "Yes. Tell them they all are wrong and that we will overcome them *now and forever.*"

Let's talk about a person who can blow up a building in Oklahoma killing over one hundred sixty-five people including children. He's sent to jail and as evil as he is, still received five marriage proposals.

God: "Sick, demented and evil.

This world *is* sick. *Now* IS *the time. Love.*"

Donna: "Let's talk about rooms."

God: "Areas where people go here and on the other side."

Donna: "For instance, jails."

God: "Hell."

Donna: "Mental institutions."

God: "A few people are close to 'God' there, others *are in* hell!"

Donna: "Holy buildings."

God: "Peace, love and caring. Where were *you* born? Where do you *allow* yourself to stay? Your home *is your* soul, clean *it* up here for the other side! For the most part you can move up, here and in heaven. It's all up to *YOU*, but you can not leave the lowest pits of hell's fire. *Love and peace!* Your home IS your soul, clean it up for the other side!

There are 'Gate Keepers' here on earth which decide who goes to heaven and who goes to hell! I am aware of all that choose ME and him, but my helper is the one who sends them where they NEED to go. The lower you are here, the lower you are there! If there is no remorse at the last minute, they will NOT come to ME.

If my helper knows the person has good intentions in his/her soul - they are allowed to intervene and put a word of love in on their behalf. Then they help that person to see the light on the earth plane, getting him or her to change their ways for the road to heaven. The Angel of The Gate will make them aware that if they don't change, their other choice is the road and rooms to and in hell! The higher you are here, the higher you are up there! Someone will also greet you in the light or at the gate to assist you to your chosen room in heaven.

In a sense you are all gate keepers with your prayers for others. Now you can see how guilty, fearful souls without prayer, and/or unbelievers could get stuck on earth."

Donna: "I think we'd better not talk badly about or to anyone. I wouldn't want to get a helper angry at me. Remember we're always being watched and tested."

Chapter 20

A Message From God To Evil: The Grey Area

This chapter took me *at least five tries* to complete. There are still some things in it that I don't understand. I have to admit I just *don't* understand, but I have to give it to you and I can't change it. The chapters before were coming a lot smoother and more quickly, especially when *I* didn't get in the way. This is a dark rainy summer day to be organizing this chapter. The last time I was trying to complete this chapter, about halfway through, it started *pouring* rain. The wind picked up, blowing things off my tables and almost blew the blinds off the windows. The crows were causing a VERY *loud* commotion, and my cat was running around the house jumping on everything, acting crazy. I had to stop recording for a couple of minutes until things calmed down. *Thank God!*

A little about Dameon, a previous acquaintance of mine (although he's been replaced by someone else who's almost as undependable): Dameon has never been married and is very close to his controlling, wealthy mother. He works as a scientist while taking classes and reading to update his profession.

He has a bad side and a good side. One minute he would be so sinful; the next he seemed *so* proper. In this case the good *could also* be Satan trying *anything* to influence you to do what *he* wants you to do. Dameon showed his ignorance by making plans with me for the whole day and then he would not show up, or call me to say he couldn't make it. We'd go for months without speaking. He would call after a while and I would say, "I don't even like you. Stop calling me." And I would hang up on him. He is a *slave* to Satan!

He would call me back to say, "I *thought* YOU would be more compassionate."

I hung up on him again and thought, "He can keep *his* evil pride and GUILT, that TRIES to control me."

God: "There *is* a reason for everything. Remember not to give up on someone BEFORE all of your lessons are learned."

Donna: "Why does he keep calling me back?"

(I realize *one* reason is the last sentence.)

God: "Dameon is one of many people who *thinks* Satan is protecting him from this cruel world. When in fact, Satan *is* creating jealousy, ego, confusion and loneliness. Dameon is also physically sick all the time because he is arrogant, self-absorbed, ignorant, miserable, and a hateful, sad, *lost* soul! Dameon makes promises that Satan does not keep!"

Donna: "A message came through to me *very clearly to see Dameon* and *speak* to Satan. THIS appointment they kept! He came into my home, sat in a chair and we proceeded to have a conversation."

God through Donna: "What came to me to ask was, 'Do you believe that God *is more powerful*?' "

Satan through Dameon: "No, we have a lot of people on this earth and beyond."

God/Donna: "So do we, that's not the point. We need to find a grey area of compromise."

Dameon: "I don't understand."

God: "I am not talking to *you*."

Dameon: (confused) "Oh."

Satan through Dameon: "Satan would think that he is winning the game if someone in a fight wants to *compromise*."

God: "There is NO winning or losing. We have to find the grey area or the world will die and we will ALL *lose*!"

Satan: "We don't care, we will have a lot of people in our house."

God: "We will have a lot of souls in our home, also. That's not the point, the *planet is dying* NO ONE WILL WIN!!!" (Said with POWER through me!)

Dameon: "I don't understand the questions."

God: "I am not talking to you!"

Satan through Dameon: "What do we have to do?"

God: "Give up your ways. You can give up some things and still be in command of your own people, but *in* love and hope for a better day here and hereafter. Stop the hate and we will love one another now and forever. AMEN. So let it be! LOVE!"

Satan: "Let the games begin. Hold onto your lessons. We will not compromise today or tomorrow. We will not leave our unholy land for you to tell us what to do here and hereafter."

Donna: "I did not feel closure with this statement."

God: "We *have* to find a grey area."

Satan: "I will think about it."

When Dameon stood up in my living room, he looked *very* confused and tired. He said he could feel my power here and did not want to be hurt.

Donna: "You will not be hurt. You can leave now. I'll talk to you later."

Dameon: "Thank you."

***

3/1/99: Just a note from Carol: I really had trouble editing this page. When I tried to type, all z's came across the whole page, also every time I tried to type "soul" it came out as "sour". As I type *this* paragraph soul comes out as "sour" *again.* These keys are on opposite sides of the keyboard and on different rows. I've never made that mistake before! Donna immediately asked Samantha to pray and things went back to normal—for a while. This whole chapter IS JINXED!

***

And so it begins. The minute Dameon left I started to write. (This is my problem chapter.)

God said right after Dameon left: "Now that he is gone, he does not believe it. We will show him. Call Dameon and leave the following message on his answering machine. Get the lesson NOW or else. *I have the power,* NOT *you!!!* Release what is fair NOW, *not* when it is too late *or* ELSE!

As happy as *I* am, is how you *will* be. As sad as I am, is how sad YOU WILL BE!!! I am not playing any more."

Satan: "As much as I laugh, is as much as you will cry."

God: "We will agree to a grey area or you will be *condemned to your hell of eternity for eternity.* BELIEVE IT!!!"

Donna: "I am not getting clear messages on this section."

Satan: "Don't bother me anymore now that *I* have lived on this unhappy earth. *It* will be my way or NO WAY!"

God: "You, evil, will compromise and find the grey area or suffer in hell for eternity, BELIEVE ME. He *flunked his* test."

Satan: "If whatever a person does to hurt someone on this earth *that's* what will happen to *them*. An eye for an eye, a tooth for a tooth."

God: *"We* WILL *get a balance. It* WILL *have to happen!!!"*

Satan: "Don't jerk me around. I will not stand for it. Believe it. Get lost and *'don't be there when I come home!'* " (*Dameon was still on the road. I was channeling Satan from his car, or was Satan still here? It took me a while to figure out what Satan's last statement meant - me being on Dameon's answering machine.*)

When Dameon arrived home, he called me back and said, "That was POWERFUL!"

I went on to write:

Satan sarcastically said, "Get the opinion of my mother, to sell the idea of *self-addressed love*. To be here now and not later." (Remember, Dameon is close to his mother who has this *same* belief system. Is that who he was talking about?!)

God: "Time to see the truth, be there *now* or else. Find the grey area, or I WILL KILL *you as* YOU *breathe,* BELIEVE IT! What do I have to say to prove it or compromise?" (This came through very secure, loud, positive, and powerful.)

Satan: "You have to sell your soul."

God: "I've just had it with you!"

(I got a very disgusted feeling.)

Note: Now the crows are back *screaming* in front of my apartment.

Satan: *"Through* a good human, that practices a lot of learning he was surprised to *hear* you, and was *alive* to you seeing his soul *being one of* YOU, *seeing him."* (*in* Dameon)

Donna: "SIGH. I saw Satan cross from left to right within Dameon's eyes."

God: "You need to be helpful with me to see our other side. To see how we live with honor."

Satan: "I am NOT SEEING THAT."

God: "To see what we need to sell our souls with people to see *how* to live better lives, and have better souls, and love. *I* can do anything, believe me. THIS is the grey area. THIS is the war ground. *No one* is winning or losing. Yes, the earth will die because of greedy, evil people like you. *You* are polluting it and you will have a lot of souls down in your house. But we will have all the good in our home. The only thing that is going to really die *is this earth.* THIS is the war ground, no one is winning or losing so let's see what can come of this new way of thinking of LOVE."

Satan: "We can go ahead and sell our souls to you and you can reprieve us to go to hell, but you have to see if we can live like you first so why don't we talk about that?"

God: "Compromise. 'Let the band begin!' The life music of being happy!"

Donna: "God, I am tired of this chapter. Please help me through this."

God: "I will if you tell them the rest, *then* it will be over."

Donna: "Weeks later I was sitting on my couch *still* trying to figure out some of these messages. Don't forget they didn't let me know *who* was speaking *when*?"

Then my phone rang, Satan/Dameon was on the other end. (He must have known I needed help).

Donna: "May I ask you a question again?"

Dameon/Satan: "Yes."

Donna: I repeated our previous conversation.

Satan: "You are asking too much that we love one another. The people YOU *created* are not capable of *that.* The HUMAN person is not capable of loving one another and they won't LOVE one another. The reason I exist is *because of hate*. I am not responsible for people's hate. *(Dameon* did not even realize that he had said 'I'). I *am* the RESULT *of people's hate*!!!" (1/99: Is he saying people feel hate and then he jumps into them?)

Donna: "How do *we* stop the hate?"

Satan said sarcastically: "God gave 'His' COMMANDments to humans. I command that you not kill anyone. *I command* that you don't do this. *I command* you don't do that. *God* never *commanded* people to LOVE *one another*. Jesus did speak of love and the devil tried to get Jesus to jump off of a mountain and if *he* was truly from God, 'HIS' ANGELS would come down from heaven to rescue him." (In a happy voice) Satan said, "*He* would not do it. I feed on hate, *take away the hate* take me away! *Take away love* and God goes away!"

Donna: "What if I asked you to jump off of the Empire State Building? Would you do it? And *don't ever* think you can treat *me that way!!!"*

Satan said sarcastically: "*Jesus never asked* Satan to do ANYTHING."

Donna: "I am asking you! And *where is the GREY area*? Why can't we have a *grey area*?" (Compromise: black and white becomes grey)

Satan: "If we were on a bus and there was just one seat left, who would get it, *love or hate*?"

Donna: "LOVE would give you the seat."

Satan: "Then you would *have to* get off the bus."

Donna asked angrily: "What next? I would *have to* leave the state? I don't think so! You do not want to compromise. Why can't you compromise?" (1/99: I'm sure some feelings crept in of being FORCED by hate to leave the city I love.)

Satan: "We are at a stand off. There are some times you don't like me but I don't think you hate me. Listen to Mozart's, 'Love and Hate Goes for a Walk'. Read up on Saint Thomas Aquinas and Saint Francis. They started out as playboys." Then, reflectively, "I don't know why, they changed their ways. If you are using this in your book you have to write *exactly* what I say and use my name or you will be committing perjury."

Donna: (I didn't know who said that. It took me off guard.) "You want me to use *your* name??"

Satan: "Yes."

Donna: "I explicitly read the pages to him and told him I said, 'Satan.' You could feel him thinking."

Then he said, "Okay!"

I also told him, "You know I don't read a lot," referring to his suggestion, "and would you just think about the question now and call me back?"

Satan: "Yes."

Satan had also said: "We believe if a man rapes a child that he can*not* be rehabilitated. You can send him to jail, then they let him walk the streets. He *will* do it again. That's what he enjoys in life, so he will do it over and over. He has to be stopped."

God/Donna: "What if we gave that person an exorcism to free him and enable him to change his ways and live a good life and after life."

Satan: "Ah! YOUR *exorcisms* (very sarcastically). There would have to be permission from the person or I don't know maybe there would not have to be permission. But he can go back to his bad ways if he did *not* give permission."

God/Donna: "Yes."

Satan: "I don't know. I will have to think about it. Let me think about it."

Satan doesn't care if you live or die, if you are *bad*, he gets you either way. But the *earlier you die* with evil in you, the better for him down below. The *longer* you live the better your chances of becoming awake and learning how to pray to GOD *before* you reach hell's fire. Satan does not want you to do that good loving deed to help each other, animals, and this planet. Satan HATES love!

Now you can see the confusion I've been going through. I waited a half hour and called Dameon/Satan back.

Donna: "Dameon, what are you doing?"

Dameon: "I am reading the paper."

Donna: "His voice was changed. I knew we would not communicate much more today. I have a short question for you. Did you think about what we talked about? Do you have an answer?"

Dameon/Satan: "Yes", he said calmly, "I think it will give your readers something to *think about*."

Donna: "We will talk again about this in the future. Then I sighed deeply."

Dameon/Satan: "Yes . . . . . What's wrong?"

Donna: "I am tired, that's all."

Dameon: "Well, look at all the work you are doing."

Donna: "Yes...That must be IT."

After I hung up I asked, "God, what should I do?"

God: "Be conscious of evil around you and be careful not to tell them ANYTHING more."

Donna: "No people, I am not scared. I *am* protected. Once you KNOW and truly trust in God you have no fear. I feel almost like I am wearing a bullet-proof body-suit.

Do you have a little fear of a friend, husband, wife or even a child? *That* is THEIR evil in and around them. Protect yourself, bless them and move on if they don't want to find the light."

A few days later Dameon called me in the afternoon. "What are you doing tonight?"

Donna: "I'm *going out around 8 P.M.*. Talk to you tomorrow."

It was a very humid day so I only had a salad for lunch, ICE CREAM for dinner, and an *apple* in front of me. I had decided to stay home and was screening my calls. *I was* BORED. By now everything I had to do that day was finished and there was nothing on television. It seems over forty years ago when there were only a few TV stations, more shows were entertaining and fun, with less repeats and violence than today. Anyway, it was about 9:30 P.M. when the phone rang. Satan, through Dameon, was coming over my answering machine. *"I am* BORED as *you* probably are *right now*. I think I'll go out and have an ICE CREAM (after a couple of seconds). No, maybe I'll just have a salad or some FRUIT!" I got the CHILLS. Satan KNEW I didn't go out AND what food I had eaten all day and night.

I called back the next day and on his machine said, "This call is for DAMEON!" I did not get a call for a few days after that. He must have been out being evil.

God: "Everyone *stop creating hate*. YOU are festering in it. You are WALLOWING and WALKING in it. YOU are creating wars in your own neighborhoods and in your own country. What is WRONG *with* YOU? STOP IT NOW before *it's* too late.

Satan's job as a salesperson is *to* LIE *to you,* ENTICE you. He gets you to TRUST in him. He tells you what he KNOWS you want to hear and *talks you into doing wrong* to get what *he wants, your* SOUL. And *if he gets to you, your soul is his*!!! *Forever!* FOREVER!!!"

Donna (with God): Dameon and I went for a walk one day but I had no idea Satan was with us until Satan said, "Look, wherever there is no shade, the weeds are green and the grass is brown."

Donna: "What does that have to do with good and evil?"

Satan answered, "The weeds get GREEDY when it rains and take ALL the water from the grass. That's a message to evil people."

I replied, "So good people are constantly pulling out weeds on a day-to-day basis, *I* would rather look at grass. (Figuratively speaking.)

Love and Hate go for a walk."

God: "PLAY *now*, PAY *later*!"

Chapter 21

#9 Thou Shalt Not Bear False Witness Against Thy Neighbors

My grandparents, on my mother's side, were from Ireland. My grandmother's maiden name was Mary McMahon. She married William Clark. Clark without the E means you came from Ireland, Clarke with the E means you came from England. My grandparents came from Ireland on the same boat with *Ed McMahon's* relatives, who were directly related to my grandmother. He's the same Ed McMahon who was on the Johnny Carson show, as well as other shows.

On Sundays after church, and holidays, Mr. and Mrs. McMahon and Ed would visit my grandparents and mother on Bridge Street in Lowell, Massachusetts (I now live off of a Bridge St.).

In 1999 I wrote a letter asking Ed what he remembered about my grandparents because I had never met them. He's the only one in the world I know of who might still remember my grandparents and mother as they were when they lived in Lowell.

February 9, 1999: Ed kindly responded to the letter I sent him. It turns out our grandparents were from County Clare, and we are related to the Boston Fitzgeralds and therefore JFK as well. He remembers at the time, everyone was *very* "Irish," including my mother.

Small world isn't it? You never know if you're related to the person next to you. It's like when you're beeping your horn angrily at someone, and it turns out to be someone you *know*. So instead of continuing to yell at them, you *pretend* you were beeping and waving at them to say, "Hi!" We all do it. Then we feel silly. Do YOU KNOW for *SURE* that we are *not* ALL related? Let's act as if we *all* HAVE the SAME common bond. OUR FATHER!

On my father's side, my English great grandmother's name was "Mary *Winchester* Howard." She was using her maiden name *with* her married name in the late 1800s. Was she ahead of her time or *did it* COME AROUND *again*?

I have some letters she wrote in 1903, (just before she passed away) to my grandfather, her son John Howard. *My Heritage*!

She mentions once living in Leicester. She writes, "*When you was a little fellow, do you remember it? It seems almost like a dream that we ever lived there*."

In another letter, this one dated Tuesday, November 3, 1903, Mary mentions giving John, her son, the *Winchester Family* "genealogy" book. Some day I hope to find a copy of the book. Unfortunately, no one in my family can remember seeing it.

A close girl friend of mine, named Glen, suggested I send my request into Yankee magazine. I did, and it was randomly chosen from MANY other requests. To make a long story short, our Winchester genealogy book has found its way home to my family as a wonderful Christmas present on December 24th, 1996 from a long, lost cousin named Al, who lives on "Harwood" Place. The book has been updated and now my name is part of the Winchester history. It's a wonderful feeling! Thank you, Glen, for all of your much appreciated spiritual support, and also thanks to God, Yankee Magazine and Al for returning the book home once again. Some things you just can't buy. If you could see all of the different names and locations in the genealogy book, you would understand what I mean about our *common bond*, and that we are all truly related. A little bit of someone's blood from *long ago* is running through our veins right now, possibly someone you would never suspect. You never know who's next to you.

Let's get back to Mary's letter. She closes with, "*Lots of love to you all. Tell, John Henry* (my father*) he is Gram's darling, good boy. Kiss both babies for Gram*. Your loving mother, *Mary Winchester Howard*."

What did I miss out on by never meeting ANY of my grandparents and by having OLDER parents? *They did the best that they could, God.*

Yvonne, Samantha and I went to town to look up the records on our family histories.

We all have so many secrets in OUR FAMILY CLOSETS. Unfortunately, a lot of other information has passed away with our ancestors. I feel sad because looking back helps me to see why I do the things I do *today*.

Our First Search

Twenty-three year old Emily is being wheeled into the delivery room of the Boston Lying-In Hospital on Tuesday, April 14, 1942. Sometime before 4 A.M. the doctor happily announced, "It's a BOY!" as he held him up for others to see.

Emily didn't remember anything after being wheeled out of the delivery room. Later that day, she thought the SEVERE HEADACHE she had was caused from lying down for such a long period of time. When she could barely lift her head off the pillow she realized that it was much more than that, and figured that she must have been given some drugs, although she didn't know why or recall when she might have received any. Unable to coordinate her body, she still managed to feed her tiny son. What seemed strange to Emily was why there were two nurses, one on each side of her, not allowing her to unwrap his blanket. The nurses did, however, assist in steadying him, so he wouldn't fall from her limp arms.

Emily was still groggy, but her deep love for children carried her to the nursery that evening. While there, she focused on her own handsome son, which gave her a warm loving feeling. She also admired his cute roommates and read ALL of their name tags. Even though she was STILL woozy, she went back a second time. After seeing him again Emily unsteadily walked back to her room and went to sleep.

The next morning, Wednesday, Emily was still, surprisingly, HEAVY-HEADED and couldn't help wondering if she had been drugged again during the night. As she was thinking this, the nurses were on their way into the room with all the babies. The nurses handed the woman in the next bed her baby first today, instead of after Emily. It was then that

Emily looked down at her hospital bracelet, and noticed the numbers were higher than they were on Tuesday. Realizing someone had obviously changed her bracelet during the night, a slow bubbling panic started to rise within her.

"What's going on?" she shrieked.

The woman in the next bed kindly tried to reassure Emily by saying, "Calm down, everything's all right. You had twins yesterday!" The nurse stood frozen in time as the woman continued, "I saw you go back into the delivery room again, after me." Then another mother in the room confirmed this fact.

The nurse handed Emily her baby girl, and after delivering all the other babies in the room, she started to leave. Emily panicked and screamed, "I WANT MY BABY! WHERE IS HE??"

The nurse, looking frightened, replied, "I'll go get the doctor."

A short while later, the doctor STORMED into the room with the nurse running along behind him.

He was shouting, "What is this? Are you saying that this is not your child?"

Emily frantically screamed, "I'm not saying any such thing. I *know* she's my child. She looks just like my husband. I now know that I had TWINS! I was given a boy yesterday and a girl today. I want both of my babies!! Where is my son?? I want him now!! I want both of my babies!!"

The doctor angrily snapped, "He's dead, and you're lucky to be taking one baby home."

Later on that day, blond-haired, blue-eyed Emily went to the nursery in search of her son, but he was nowhere to be found. Yet she remembered that her baby son also resembled his blond-haired, blue-eyed father.

After Emily and her husband, named Trygve, left the hospital with their little girl, who was born with blue eyes and brown hair (which after only a month turned light blond), they contacted the hospital every day to pick up their son's body for burial, but the hospital personnel couldn't find his body. It occurred to Emily, her doctor never told her she was having twins, and no one seems to know where her baby girl had been hidden for the first day of her life. You just never think it's going to happen to *you*, especially coming from an upper middle class family.

The authorities came to their home day after day asking questions, but to no avail. The "black market" adoption agency had once again won.

"Make it easier on yourself and your family," the authorities said, "always speak of him as if he were dead."

The father, who didn't like to lie, promised his wife that he would never speak of it again. NEVER!

Seven years later the authorities came to their door. Emily, in GREAT EXCITEMENT, called to her husband, expecting good news from the search. Instead, they were told the seven year limit had been reached on a missing person, and the search had to be given up. As a result, the mother internalized her grief, allowing it to fester until it eventually created a poison in herself and toward her daughter...Samantha.

I could feel, as Samantha told me her story, her new found pain of realization. Sam was forty nine years old when her seventy two year old mother told her that her twin brother is possibly still *alive today*. Sam was in a state of shock for about a year and a half after hearing the truth.

By the way, we found NO birth certificate or death certificate for Samantha's brother.

You never think it's going to happen to *you*!

***

Yvonne came with us because she knew how to do the research. A woman named Angela, needed some records looked up in town. Yvonne was kind enough to offer to help her as well.

Our Second Search

Angela was a young woman in her twenties, when on May 15, 1967, at 6 A.M., she was wheeled into the delivery room on an emergency basis at the Boston Lying-In Hospital.

The nurses kept telling her, "You're not in labor, you're not in labor."

Angela cried, "But I'm in so much pain. Why am I in so much pain? Save my baby and let me die instead."

A nurse, mocking her, said: "Save my baby and let me die instead."

As Angela's pain continued, so did the medication. So much medication was given to Angela that she passed *out* cold. The doctor on duty proceeded to take care of her until her own doctor arrived.

She awoke twenty-four hours later in the recovery room with a nurse shaking her, saying: "Wake up, you have a baby boy, wake up."

Sometime later Angela, still extremely groggy, could hardly make out what the male attendant was asking her.

He asked, "Would you like to go see your son before you go back to your room?"

"Yes," she said softly. Two attendants wheeled her to two nurseries on two different floors *to no avail*. They could not seem to find her son anywhere.

The next morning on his rounds, the doctor came into her room, talking a mile a minute like everything was normal. Angela said to him jokingly, "Is my baby so ugly that you are hiding him from me?"

The doctor looked quickly down at the floor. "You had a stillborn." Still not making eye contact with her, he said, "God did you a favor."

That afternoon around feeding time, a nurse came in and asked Angela, "Where's your baby?"

Confused, Angela replied, "What baby? There is no baby."

The nurse became outraged and angrily asked, "Where's your baby? I have to bring him back to the nursery. Give him to me," as if Angela was hiding him.

Angela somberly said, "There is no baby." The irate nurse stormed out of the room. Angela was so confused. One nurse would give her a pill to dry up the milk, and another nurse would come in every feeding time to retrieve the baby for the nursery.

The second day the doctor came in jabbering away again asking her questions. Angela, still incoherent, could hardly respond. The doctor asked angrily, "What's the matter with *you*?" Before her still-drugged brain had a chance to respond, he was over next to her bed picking a glass up from her bed stand. As he was smelling it, he asked, "What's in this?"

Weakly she replied, "Apple juice."

The following day, as she was preparing to leave the hospital, she said to her mother, "I have a baby SOMEWHERE in this hospital, but no one is approaching me about having the body buried. What's going on? After all, this *is* a baby hospital."

Her mother said, "I'll go see what's happening." A long time passed before her mother returned with a woman who worked in the office. The woman had a stack of papers in her hand.

"Please sign these," she said.

A still groggy Angela asked, "What are they for?"

The woman replied, "We use a local funeral home. He buries all of our still-born babies for us at a fee of forty-five dollars. Your mother has already paid in full."

Even though Angela could hardly keep her eyes focused, she noticed that there was a green sheet of paper on top of two blue copies and some white papers underneath which looked like legal documents. Angela recognized this because she was working for a lawyer, at the time, who *happened to suggest* she use this doctor. She was very skeptical but still in a dream-state of drugs, and in a perfect world she would have read all of these documents twice and not signed any of them until she understood every word. But THIS is NOT a perfect world. Angela, in slow motion, started lifting her arm up to sign.

God kept saying to her, "What are the blue papers ... what are the blue papers???"

Her drugged brain would not allow her seemingly cemented mouth to ask the question. She just wanted to put this awful experience behind her, so Angela heavy-heartedly, signed. As the stranger walked out of the room with her papers, Angela asked herself loudly, "*What did I sign?* WHAT DID I JUST SIGN???"

That question still haunts her to this day.

A short while later, a bill came to her home from the Boston Lying-In Hospital. The bill was for her baby boy who was in the nursery for FIVE days. Angela was only in the *Living-Hell* hospital for *three* days. Angela could take no more. She was upper middle class Italian and very family orientated. Every day that passed she wondered if he looked like his father, who had blond hair and blue eyes. Now she has this bill dilemma to add to her continuing miseries. In a daze, Angela rushed to the hospital. Once at the office, she asked, "What's going on here? I was told my baby was stillborn."

A very business-like woman said, "All our records show you had a baby boy in this nursery for five days and you owe us this money." Angela couldn't get through to any of the "healers" in this hospital. They didn't know how to find her baby, but they sure did know how to send out a bill, which, by the way, she never paid.

She went home and called the funeral parlor where her son supposedly had been taken. The funeral director said he had never heard of her before. She persistently called him. "Have you found any of my records or any new information for me?"

"No," he kept on insisting angrily. Now you can see her dilemma. She could get no answers. It was about a month later that a friend drove her to the cemetery. Angela could not go alone. You see, the stress was just too much for her to bear, for fear of what she might or might not find. Her friend went into the cemetery office and discovered that there was a card with her name, baby boy and a plot number on it. As they drove to the plot, her heart was beating so loudly that she could hear it. Every second was torture. The closer to the plot, the more physically sick she became. Once there, she stared mournfully out from the car window and down at the ground...that had *never been opened.*

Angela was totally discouraged and could take no more of going around in circles. She was *so tired* and *so depressed* that she finally reached her breaking point. As a result, she suffered a nervous breakdown and spent time in a hospital.

If *she* couldn't find him he just wasn't there. A year later she called the funeral director again to no avail. Angela had to leave it all behind her now.

In June of 1974, Angela was having her second baby on the same floor of the same hospital. Her husband said to her, "I know how much losing the first baby means to you, so I'm going to the office and look up your records." But there were *no records* of Angela *ever* having been in the hospital that *lies-in Boston.*

After being a widow for many years, Angela was planning to remarry. It was a cold, cloudy day at dusk when she decided to look for some sort of closure. So she drove half-heartedly to the cemetery to visit the empty plot one last time, only to find it eerily surrounded by weathered, mournful teddy bears watching over someone else's child.

"I was *so tired* and *so depressed* and I could get no answers."

By the way, we found NO birth certificate or death certificate for Angela's son.

NOTE: The Universal Standard Encyclopedia states that the Boston Lying-In Hospital opened in 1832, merged in 1966 with the Free Hospital for Women, then with the Boston Hospital for Women. Definition: *lying* means the telling of a lie; *lying-in* means confinement in childbirth. Lying in hospital!

I watched a TV program called Leeza which told of a Dr. Hicks from Georgia, who illegally put a lot of children up for adoption and had their birth certificates altered, sealed or buried. It did help some women who felt they could not care for their babies.

Samantha saw a series on "Unsolved Mysteries," about Bessie Bernard and her father selling "Black Market Babies," in the United States. The births were mostly recorded in New York. The *birth dates* were changed by days, weeks, and sometimes even months. The *birth parents'* names were also changed. Bessie's father escaped, avoiding prosecution. Bessie paid a fine, but never spent one day in prison.

Georgia Tan placed around 5,000 orphans on the "Black Market" in Memphis, Tennessee. Ethyl Nation was another who stole children for adoption. Even today, it still goes on.

***

When Samantha was around twenty-four years old, she lived with her family at 389 Marlborough St., in Boston. While coming home from work in the warm weather, about three times a week for a few weeks, she would see the same two young men standing and talking together in front of the house next door. Each time she would hear a soft, very kind voice, calmly insisting, "Turn around, your twin brother is here! You can reach right out and touch him!!" Samantha thought she was losing her mind. Her mother had always told her that her twin brother had only lived one day, and died sometime during the night, so she stubbornly refused to turn around and take a good look. Within nine years the realization sadly hit her when Samantha had a near death experience. While in the "Tunnel of Light" she heard the SAME, soft, very kind voice, urgently say to her, "Stop, you must go back and take care of your children." She looked around to see if someone else was there, because she only had one child. Not understanding, Sam continued on into "The Light" and was stopped again, and the same voice repeated, "Stop, you *must* go back and take care of your children." She again did not realize this message was meant for her, and was about to go on again towards "The Light" when suddenly, the tunnel sped away from her at GREAT SPEED, quickly vanishing out of sight - but not out of mind. Now, having had more children, like the voice had mentioned, she realizes she should have listened to that kind voice many years ago on Marlborough St., and done as she was told.

Samantha prays daily to the Lord, asking Him for the help she needs to find her twin brother.

Samantha's birth name was V. G. Stensrud. Born April 14, 1942. Her brother has blue eyes and may still have blond hair. They are of Norwegian heritage.

We will NEVER stop our search!

***

We are going to my search next, but it pales in comparison to Samantha's and Angela's searches. I feel totally depleted just writing those stories. They are living them!

Our Third Search

First of all, let me say that I was brought up in an English and Irish Catholic family believing NO ONE in my family was EVER divorced, but lately it seems everyone I meet has a SECRET CLOSET!

My father retired when I was in high school. He never went out, which was eventually his ruin. He mainly sat around watching the news, baseball games, and did a lot of reading, especially the stock reports. He taught me a lot at a very young age, about water pollution, food and housing shortages due to over-population, and the dangers of coming earthquakes. Cautiously, he always paid cash for everything.

On one particular morning, I was ill and stayed home from school. As my father slept in the back part of our large house on Adams Street, he had no way of knowing that I was still home. I was awakened later that morning by screams echoing through our old Victorian house, "That's not *my* credit card. It's my first wife's card."

As I was lying upstairs in bed, I was dumbfounded, to say the least, but there are no coincidences or accidents in life. I did not speak to him or anyone else about that day, which I now regret, but I was brought up to keep my mouth shut and never ask personal questions. I always had a feeling there was another brother somewhere.

Getting back to our day of record searches in town, my friends and I looked up my father's first marriage. I then looked up births to see if I might have siblings from the first marriage. There he was, "Joseph Charles Howard." I was *very* excited. Samantha and Yvonne helped me to look through marriages for Joseph...nothing. Then we looked through the books containing death certificates...nothing. After that day, Yvonne drove me to the Registry of Motor Vehicles. They checked back ten years. No driver's license or tickets were found. If he had used someone else's car and was stopped, it would have shown up on the computer. I went to the social security office but the woman led me to believe she could not find him in the computer. It was like he had fallen off the face of this earth.

— our CIRCLES in life —

We also discovered my grandfather, John Howard, divorced his first wife, leaving children behind. They might have been from HER first marriage. These records were old, torn, hard to read and some were missing. Then he married his parent's IRISH SERVANT, Mary Starr. Well, you can *only* IMAGINE how *thrilled his mother,* Mary Winchester Howard, and the rest of the wealthy English family were. They would not even let my pretty Irish grandmother, from

Galway, be buried in their old family cemetery plot. They even went so far as to erase her name from our genealogy book. THAT *was* an interracial marriage in the late 1800s. I'm assuming that they were married by the justice of the peace. My grand-dad, John, was forty-six when my father was born. My grandparents, John and Mary, had six children, three girls and three boys together, with only two surviving. Grandfather was born into a lot of old money. My great-grandfather, Henry and great-grandmother, Mary Winchester Howard, had six children, three girls and three boys. I share the same birthday with one of their daughters. My great-*great* grandfather, John Jr. and great-great grandma Priscilla Cheever Howard had five children, three girls and two boys. Yes, old money.

My father, John, divorced a Mary after a short marriage, leaving behind a child. My father was married by the justice of the peace to my pretty *Irish* mother who had cleaned houses. My father's family was not thrilled with the way his life was going. I was born when he was forty-seven, John and Margaret had five children three girls and two boys. Dad was also wealthy as a child.

Sound familiar? CIRCLES!

I am sure, regrettably, there are more ironies which I might never learn about.

Also I *was* married for a *short* while to an Irish man in my later years, leaving behind a stepson. We were married by the justice of the peace because he was divorced. My father did all right later on, but I was certainly not born into money. My two brothers also married pretty Irish girls, who held office jobs. John and Mary have five wonderful children, three girls and two boys, and my other brother and his wife also have five wonderful children, three girls and two boys.

***

General Oliver Otis Howard, who was white, tried to help the Indians with their treaty just before they were forced to go to Tulsa, Oklahoma. General Howard fought at Gettysburg and Bull Run. He was the same Oliver Otis Howard who was very active in the founding of Howard University in

Washington, D.C. in 1867. He served as president of that institution from 1869 to 1874. The irony is that over one hundred twenty-seven years ago Oliver was helping ALL minorities even though, at that time, it was not the popular thing to do. He stood up and was counted. What would YOU have done and what would YOU do TODAY?

Now, in the late 1990's, the world watched as some students at Howard University (which is ninety-five percent black and difficult to get in to) stood up and cheered when O.J. Simpson was found innocent by a jury which was guilty of using poor judgment, just because he was a black man who was rich and famous. He and his lawyers promised NEVER to use the race card, but at least one lied, and he even made a racial remark regarding Hitler.

O.J.'s white ex-wife was found brutally butchered, along with a Jewish, male acquaintance, while her two beautiful children slept inside her home. Her faithful, heartsick dog, splattered with blood, sought help from a neighbor. Their blood was found mingled with O.J.'s blood, and DNA in his vehicle, in his home and at the crime scene. Almost $9,000 cash was found in his Bronco, but O.J. said he had only $3.63. O.J. said he cut himself, but doesn't remember how. The chances of the DNA matching between two people, which his did, is one in one hundred fifty million people. He also had scratches on him and covered himself with lies. *If the shoe fits, wear it.*

His neighbors and Hollywood friends have not spoken to him since, although it was rumored that some black actors were funding his large defense bills, but wanted to keep it secret from the whites. Perhaps these actors thought the bad luck karma wouldn't find them or their children if it were not spoken aloud.

Well anyway, I guess, it stopped more rioting in L.A.- *Lost Angels* - where *some* blacks pilfered from, beat up, and killed some white people, Asians, and whoever, because someone filmed a black man, Rodney King, being beaten up by police, and the police were judged as only doing their job. The media never showed what he had done to the police just prior to the beating. The police should not have done that evil act. They took their job and authority one step too far, but the blacks should not have used that as an excuse to act in such an *evil* way as they also did when Martin Luther King was killed. During the L.A. riots, some evil black people pulled a white man out of his truck and beat him up, crushing his skull and leaving him for dead. Four God-like blacks then risked their lives by rushing to his rescue, saving his life. One of the men, who tried to kill this white man, was caught on video, yet still was set free. I couldn't believe my ears when someone from the N.A.A.C.P. got on TV and said that the L.A. riots were the *white* people's fault. I was HOME that day, I didn't MAKE *anyone* do *anything.* By the way, Rodney King, who was beaten by police, received about one million dollars because of the beating. Since then he has been in and out of jail several times. One reason he was arrested again was because he beat up a woman. Where were the video cameras then??? I wonder if he paid her a million dollars!! The scarred-for-life white man lost his lawsuit and was given no money or satisfaction.

How ironic! One is cheered, one rewarded, and all three released.

Don't use race as an excuse for inappropriate behavior!
GOD: "What's wrong with this picture?"

...Oliver Otis Howard had a lot of dreams. He was an amazing person who was way ahead of his time. We could use more people like him today. Despite all of General Howard's efforts, the Indian treaty was not honored and the Apache Indians were forced to move to Tulsa, Oklahoma (per the Learning Channel).

My slender, pretty sister, Dorothy Howard Doss, who had beautiful, long, red hair, went on a blind date and met a wonderful, handsome man named Olin DeVerne Doss, Jr.

Dee, as he was known, was a crewman on a destroyer docked in Boston. He was part Choctaw and Cherokee Indian as well as other nationalities.

On September 28, 1952, I was the flower girl at Dee and Dorothy's wedding at Saint Leo's Church, in Dorchester. Dorothy *reluctantly and temporarily* moved from Boston to Tulsa, Oklahoma more than forty-five years ago. We were saddened by the distance which separated us from our loved ones.

As of February 1999, Dorothy and Dee have six wonderful children, ten grandchildren, three great grandchildren, with another on the way and "much" *love.*

It's like having *mixed* marriages for *peace* between the English, Irish, Indians, Blacks, Jews, Italians, Greeks, Asians, on and on *and on* ... 'till *finally*...as ONE... the GREY area becomes part of the solution.

We all meet for reasons, whether in family, neighbors, friends, work or marriage. Learn the reasons.

GOD: "How many times were the commandments broken in this chapter and *how many* commandments were broken?"

By the way, February 4, 1997, was judgment day for O.J. Nicole and Ron's families brought a wrongful death suit, a civil case, against O.J.. They won, and the jury agreed that the family should receive $8,500,000; whether they ever get it is another story. Of course the *troublesome* media said, "Let's not have any racial problems," as they brought up and showed a clip of Rodney King being beaten by the police over and *over* again. I think one saving grace was that the President of the United States was on television with a wonderful black representative from Oklahoma when O.J.'s verdict was announced. He (the Rep.) spoke about good family values, honesty, hard work, love and God.

A few days later, O.J. was fined twenty-five million in punitive charges, half for Nicole Brown's family and half for Ron Goldman's family. The same day while O.J. was on a golf course, as a cameraman was innocently filming him, O.J. attacked him with a golf club - "a time bomb."

In 2/17/99 an auction was held in which O.J.'s personal memorabilia were sold. Some people bought them and burned them in the street to protest his acquittal, no one was hurt.

4/14/99: O.J. was attacked by a well dressed man as he came off of the golf course. The man said, " I hear you have a lot of money." O.J. grabbed the gun away from him, then chased him in his vehicle and called the police. The irony is the last time he was on the cell phone to the same police, HE was being *chased* by the police. What goes around...

The number of murders committed in the United States of America in 1994 was twenty-three thousand three hundred and five. Out of that figure eight hundred twenty-three women were murdered by their husbands.

6/99: It was on TV that a man who had a black father and white mother said the Dean of Howard University would not let him in, due to the fact that his mother was white.

"God, please keep all of these people and their families in your heart, and pray the murderers save their souls from eternal hell, and also please forgive the students from Howard University who are guilty of poor judgment. Please allow them to open their hearts as General Oliver Otis Howard did"

"Rest In Peace Oliver."

***

Getting back to all my old, rich relatives. Don't ask me where all the money went. I never saw *any* of it! But no one can take my great history away from me or my DNA.

In our family we also have "The Howard Book." This book is our genealogy from the early 1720's, when Abraham

Howard came to the United States from England. He settled in Marblehead, Massachusetts, where he bought a house. The strange part of *that* is Abraham had married Frances Tarrant, the recent widow of George Tarrant who originally *owned* the house that Abraham Howard bought. In other words, Frances "came with the house." Of course, they courted a respectable amount of time before marrying. The women were SMART in *those* days!

Anyway, our family owned ships that brought trade from all over the world into the ports of Salem, Massachusetts. There is also a Howard Street and Howard House in the historical section of Salem. I have since learned that there is a Winchester Street in Coolidge Corner, named after our Winchester side of the family, because they had owned many acres there years ago. I also learned I had a great grandfather who was an officer in the Revolution. I'm very proud of my heritage, although all this and a dollar-thirty will get me a small cup of coffee.

Before Abraham came to the United States of America, he had been on an English ship called the "Dover" and was taken as a *slave* by Algerian pirates. Years later, a treaty was signed by the King of England and ransom was paid for Master Abraham Howard and the seamen from the "Dover." King George I ordered them to parade through Leicester Square in London for his personal examination in their *Turkish* SLAVE *Costumes and* long beards. Abraham's only daughter, Elizabeth, could not distinguish which one was her father — they looked so much like Turks.

There has been evidence of *white slavery* as far back as history goes, about 4,000 years in Egypt and Rome. Greece captured people during times of war, enslaving the white women. Dancing was one of their duties. Some powerful black tribes attacked weaker black tribes and over the years, captured thousands of prisoners, selling the prisoners to the Arabs who in turn sold them to the Europeans. Some black people actually owned black slaves themselves. There are still slaves *today*. Some of the women would fight with each other for the attention of their owners. There was a story on TV about one particular slave, who was haunting a house down South. This slave had poisoned one dish at supper, because the master, whom she truly cared for, turned his attention to another slave girl and was giving this slave presents. Her jealously killed his two children. The master, however, survived because he didn't eat that particular dish. These slaves had no thought that they were willingly committing adultery in the wife's home. Some people came to better lives.

History identifies, "indentured servants," who were people who *willingly* signed a contract to serve their owners for a period of TWENTY *years,* just for the passage to a new world. It was like slavery. That is also in the *past.*

Hank Pasquerella, a history major and a teacher of history (since retired) in a Boston area high school, strongly suggests that a great deal of information concerning slavery has come under recent attack. An attempt has been made to rewrite history for social purposes rather than historical purposes. In other words, some of this information came from the *old history* books — now someone is *rewriting history!!!*

Hank went on to talk to me about Salem, Massachusetts and Europe where *countless* numbers of innocent people were condemned as witches, brutally tortured; and many were put to death in the late 1600's.

One day my other sister, who looks like the actress Doris Day, and I visited an historical site in Salem. The tour guide mentioned that we had *white* slaves as well as black slaves in Boston. I never knew that! Eighty percent of all those caught harboring slaves were SET FREE by the courts. Also, it was a law that after *seven* years *all* slaves of all colors had to be set free. They were given two outfits (in those days that was like receiving a closet full of clothes) and fifty acres of land!!! FIFTY ACRES - WHERE DO I SIGN UP?

I get a lot of my information from teachers whom I have met as an adult, by calling Libraries, and by watching the Learning Channels. I recently saw on one of the Learning Channels, a documentary about *The Great Irish Famine.* (I can't *believe* I was never taught this years ago.) The famine started in 1845. At least a million Irish people starved to death. The English records were not entirely clear on that point.

There was a fungus that killed all of Ireland's potatoes. While the English were trying to decide whether to send them corn or not, the Irish were dying. And yet, food was still being sent *from* Ireland TO England. You see, the British *owned* the land in Ireland, with the exception of a few Irish Protestants who could afford to buy land from the English. But I am told that most of them did not even help their Irish Catholic neighbors. The Irish suffered an appalling life. The English had "Irish-serfs" - they were like slaves to the land. The English also considered the Irish to be poor, low life, dirt farmers (keep in mind that I am of English and Irish descent) and treated them as if they were THEIR *slaves*, taking care of THEIR *land,* renting the farms from THEM. If the Irish didn't produce enough potatoes to sell, they would have no money for the English landlords. As a result, they would be thrown out of their own homes, off the farms of their blood, sweat and tears, to either become beggars in town or come to the United States to start a new life. No wonder my Irish mother bragged so much to strangers about her daughter who owned a new house by the water. It took me a long time to figure out she was bragging, because she never told me she was proud of me. I guess she did, in her own way, although it was not in her *nature* to do so. The Irish had to fight hard for what they got. I did it for myself, anyway, not for praise.

But I digress - A large number of Irish emigrated to America at the time of "the famine". In 1847 about five thousand Irish were quarantined on Deer Island, which was very small. Some poor souls actually arrived with green around their mouths from eating grass, because they were so poor and hungry.

About eight hundred Irish died on Deer Island, and now they lay next to a sludge treatment plant.

May they rest in peace.

This one's for you!

Oh, Danny boy, the pipes, the pipes are calling,
From glen to glen and down the mountain side,
The summer's gone and all the flowers are dying,
'Tis you, 'tis you must go and I must bide.

But come you back when Summer's in the meadow,
Or when the valley's hushed and white with snow,
'Tis I'll be there in sunshine or in shadow,
Oh, Danny boy, oh Danny boy, I love you so.

And if you come when all the flowers are dying,
And I am dead, as dead I well may be,
You'll come and find the place where I am lying,
And kneel and say an 'Ave' there for me.

And I shall hear, tho' soft you tread above me,
And all my dreams will warm and sweeter be,
If you will not fail to tell me that you love me,
Then I simply sleep in peace, until you come to me.

***

Words and music by: "Fred E. Weatherly"- 1913

Bag pipes were used to spread news of war, etc.
Glen: is a secluded narrow valley.
Bide: Means to stay.
Ave: Means Hail, as in Hail Mary!

Top of the morning to you.
And the rest of the day to you!

The Irish were greeted with hate, prejudice and ridicule by the Protestant, English and Dutch peoples who told them they were a disgrace to humanity and worse than peasants. These people suppressed the Irish by keeping them out of the nicer areas of town. No one would give the Irish jobs. Signs were put up everywhere that read "*No Irish* ALLOWED," *and* "NO IRISH NEED APPLY." They were not allowed in most restaurants, bars and some stores. Closer to our time, the KKK burned a cross against the Irish in the Chestnut Hill area of Boston. Sad, but true. As a result of all this, the Irish had to live in slums and when their money ran out, they were thrown out into the gutters. Yet they *persisted, got jobs and made something of themselves.*

God: "If someone pushes you down, YOU have to *get up* and find *another avenue to* SUCCEED!"

Donna: "Not once have I ever met an Irish or English person who has called me sister just because we are the same nationality."

God: "We are *all* brothers and sisters."

Not once has any Irish person *ever* said to me, including members of my family, "I was *suppressed* by the English!" YOU can only suppress YOURSELF!

My loyalty is *where I live* - "America" - by my choice, *without* losing my attachment to MY *roots*.

My knowledge of MY history, *here and over* THERE, IS *power and freedom* FOR ME.

This is MY *her-story* and heritage of slavery and our Irish Holocaust. We've all been there and done it. NOW let us learn from it, let it go and let God, otherwise we can not go forward to be the *best people* we can be.

"God shed His grace on thee,
And crown thy good with brotherhood
From sea to shining sea!"
(America, the Beautiful by Katharine Lee Bates)

People around the world are praying, dreaming, and dying to come to this promised land...America. So love us all or leave us now.

Mr. President, I saw a sad billboard recently asking for donations to end the homelessness of elderly citizens who have paid taxes all their lives. How can you send billions of our tax dollars overseas and give new incoming foreigners more benefits, including medical care, than people in the

United States of America who need them as much or more. Make these foreigners pay back the money "given" to them, as students do with college loans. I know Americans who have had triple and quintuple bypasses who could not get on S.S.I., or receive food stamps for their families, yet you hand it to healthy strangers, no questions asked. I couldn't get on S.S.I. even though I was "dying" a couple of years ago from a distended stomach filled with toxins. I also have no medical insurance. Friends of mine wanted to know, who's idea was it to put that sign on the Statue of Liberty. France? "Give us your TIRED *and* Your POOR! WE couldn't be *that* stupid, but they could be that smart! A lot of us after taxes are pretty TIRED AND POOR OURSELVES!! And after all our hard work, *we* could possibly be *homeless*. Give US some of your wealthy! Also millions, maybe even billions are spent a year on Government research Programs such as: Gore's project, or One hundred thousand dollars spent on finding out why Vidalia onions bring tears to your eyes when you cut into them. Now I'm not saying that information might not come in handy some day. I am saying to put such tests as these on hold, and put the money towards getting OUR OWN elderly off of our streets including our children and ANY animals that need help. This brings tears to my eyes! This is our Government's responsibility, it's our land! Our money should go towards that! Let's feed them all while we are at it. I'm sure this is just an oversight on the Government's part. I'm not saying not to help other countries, I'm saying to clean up *our home* first! This should go on the top of your list. I would suggest, down the road when you find some *extra* money, you can go ahead and do this type of research, but for now WE need it.

Please bring our Prisoners of Wars home at any expense.

Please don't ever forget our M.I.A.'s!

GOD .. *Bless* America!

I have been fortunate enough to meet a wonderful spiritual couple who are TRI-blooded, black, Indian and white. They have *beautiful,* GOD LOVING SOULS and love *everyone* they meet. My spiritual friend mentioned a story about "passing". A lot of white people, like myself, have no idea what that means. One day her mother told her that if she ever saw her cousin walking down the street, she should not say, "Hi!," to her because she is "passing" for white. That story amazed me. She could not even approach her as a friend, much less a relative. How lonely, to willingly give up your whole loving family. She missed out on having a wonderful, caring cousin...my friend. But I am not walking in her shoes. I don't know what she has gone through in her life. I am not judging her. People have a right to do whatever they want to make themselves happy, as long as it doesn't hurt anyone else. But I just can not fathom what life would be like to live such a lie. Did society back then affect her decision to recreate her life and pass for white, or would she still have done so today? I am sure some still pass for white, although perhaps not as many. Some blacks would have made it difficult for her to live among them because she was so pale and they would not have known she was black unless she told them or unless a relative said, "Hi."

Anyway, she told me how difficult it was when they wanted to buy a house years ago. I would LOVE to have her as my neighbor or relative. I told her how I was chased down the street several times in Roxbury and North Dorchester by *gangs* of black kids, sometimes with sticks. I also told her that when I was a school bus driver, a black girl no older than eight told me, "My *mother* said that I can do whatever I want to you because *white* people are *stupid* and are *afraid* of us, since *we* can FIGHT harder and win." That little girl LOST at a very young age. I wonder whatever happened to her and her mother? The saddest part of the incident for me was that she was living on Norwell Street, the street where I was BORN.

Because of her mother, my heritage from that part of my life is *filled with hate* instead of LOVE. (I was extremely surprised at how *overwhelmed* I became by the loss I felt when this was being typed. Tears came to my eyes as something was awakened and released deep in my soul.) I can never see my childhood homes and schools again because they were all destroyed from abuse and lack of care, and were eventually torn down. Believe it or not the white people were blamed.

It was a very dangerous area to be driving through during the riots caused by school integration. When I went back to the office one day, I learned that five minutes before I drove through a bad area, another of our station wagons, driven by a white woman, was rolled over by blacks, even though all the special needs children in the car were black. She and the children ran into a Fire Station for help and protection just in time. What were those people thinking? I don't remember seeing any of THOSE stories on TV. To this day I try to avoid that area of town because of the danger.

Similar things happened to me a few times but, thank God, I drove the school car or bus to a safer street and area. One time in particular pops into my mind: While coming off of a peninsula, I had to stop because the way was blocked by a car with an elderly white man in it. He was frightened because a lot of angry black girls and boys were beating on his car, and were in a line blocking the road directly in front of him. As I pulled up close and revved the engine, he managed to evade them. But they quickly blocked the road in front of my school car, obviously very angry that the older man had escaped from them, and as a result some of them tried to break our windows. Out of concern for the children in my school car, I accelerated in reverse. This made the kids angrier. As they ran around to the back of the car to prevent me from moving, I waited for the right moment then accelerated forward and escaped. As it turned out, the little boy seated behind me was the cousin of one girl who was hitting HIS window with a stick. She didn't even notice him. What EVIL got into her?

In the United States of America, blacks make up a little more than ten percent of the population, yet EVERY TIME I turn on the television, I hear what an awful person *I* AM *just because the color of* MY *skin is* WHITE.

I had an awakening experience in a snooty restaurant, I went out to eat with a very sick, *overweight*, white man to give him some healing messages. An older woman was sitting across from us talking a little too loudly, bragging about someone I happen to know. I just happened to look up at the same time she did, so she lowered her voice saying, "I'll tell you later," to her two friends. Then looking at the person I was with, she asked the man at her table with his back to us, to move his chair a bit, apparently to block her view from my client. My surprise and anger lasted far too long. I learned a lot from that experience. I asked God what this was about, and God said to me what if you were black, what would you have thought? The first thing I would have thought was she was being ignorant to us because we were black. When the truth of the matter is, she was just plain ignorant! Please don't *automatically* think someone is doing something to you because of the color of your skin. Research it a little further and learn from it. It might have been something you *said* or *did* to that person. If it's just coming from old ignorant prejudices, you might create *more negativity* for yourself if you don't just forget about it and let go, let God. Tell yourself they're looking at you because you're so *good* looking!

2/12/99: On TV it was announced that we are having a black history month. Do we have Native American history month or a "white" history month? Can we even say, "White History?" What's up with that??? Is THAT *equality*? There was a black comedian on "Comedy Central" every other word was *bleep white, bleep white.* Some of the jokes were funny; the swears were not. The joke that disturbed me was, "If we had a black vice-president, the blacks would *kill* the white President." The comedian said he would do it himself to be a hero. What a sick evil joke. You can tell a joke about my English or Irish heritage to me as long as it's not vicious.

I turn off *any* show which tries to divide us by mentioning color of any sort and I don't buy ANY of the sponsor's products. I grew up with BLACK *prejudice* against whites and I am SICK *of always hearing about white prejudice against blacks. Sometimes it's just to acquire things they can't otherwise get. People like that* are insulting my intelligence. It goes without saying, this does not apply to God loving and honest blacks. I feel all colors can be good at jobs even though they can't pass a written test, like me with A.D.D.! Of course I'm not talking about brain surgery, unless Edgar Cayce, the sleeping prophet & healer, is performing the operation. Be fair to 'ALL.' We can talk about race without being considered racist, I'm talking about the facts of MY life! I'm not saying it's not out there for all of us. I am saying that I'm sick of hearing about it, as a lot of other people are. I also told this dear friend *(who is like family to me)* how I protected a VERY SCARED little light skinned girl from her darker skinned schoolmates who were hitting her and calling her a "WHITE DOG" and me the "H" word, "HONKIE". What does HONKIE mean anyway?

I also told my good friend how I lost my job to a black woman, *just because I am* WHITE. Some of the black mothers did not want me telling their children to sit down and behave on the school bus because of *my color, never taking into consideration the dangers on the road,* not to mention their children's possible prejudiced future! I wonder what the *teachers* are going through?

A white friend of mine who lived in a project in Roxbury (because her family always lived in a house in that area) came home one night only to be greeted by a gang of blacks who proceeded to beat her up. As she laid on the cold cement floor in the dark corner of the hallway she begged for her baby's life screaming, "I'M PREGNANT PLEASE STOP." Instead of stopping they proceeded to kick her in the stomach. If you find yourself looking for EXCUSES as to WHY these blacks did this - I want you to pinch yourself as hard as possible, then multiply the pain by a million while picturing several sets of feet kicking your unborn child. You should also be sentenced to live in a dangerous section of town, so you can experience what's really going on and, face the facts. Then tell the next person you see that you fear the reality of life! If it had just been one person my friend would have won, as she had many times before, but it is usually a gang of roving cowards that attacks one person.

6/99, 1:13 P.M.: I took a very elderly woman to a store near her home, which borders with a dangerous section of town. On the way out of the small store, I had a *strange feeling* and looked behind me. Two well dressed, black, young guys were *very* close to us. I said, "Thanks for being so patient because we're walking so slow, you can go around us." One very adamantly and sarcastically kept refusing, saying oh *no* YOU go. As we exited the second door I *felt pressured* to move more quickly, but instead was forced by my angel to stop and turn again - this time they were almost on top of us. I grabbed her arm to protect her and stared at them, strangely she *also* said nothing. Now they looked as if they didn't know how to proceed, and they and I all stood staring at each for what seemed like forever. I felt as if I was out of body in a parallel universe or something and someone else had taken me over. While they were acting impatiently behind us, I looked around and even though the parking lot had some cars in it, and there were warning signs of having security cameras every few feet, there was no one around to help us. I felt like a deer caught by a vicious animal or a hunter, but I KNEW I was not to budge. I had noticed before they had no shopping bags in their hands and I remembered I had not seen them in the store or at the checkout counters. Yet something was keeping me calm. They finally moved off to their left when a car sped into the parking lot and stayed about five car lengths away from us. The guy behind the wheel stared at them with a look on his face like WHAT HAPPENED?? The one who spoke to us before just looked at him and shrugged his shoulders as they slowly walked in his direction. I thought I would just consider it over with but, the next day I could not let it go. I called the manager of the store who treated It nonchalantly. He has no idea why his sister store in the suburbs does not have those warning signs, which did not surprise me. There is so much stealing from people and the stores in the inner-city that a lot of the stores are closing down. One mother was caught teaching her daughter how to steal.

When are you going to learn about God? Those two uneducated evil guys didn't get a chance to rob us but they did steal my peace of mind!

I had a black friend in Roxbury who had two children. The father of the children wouldn't marry her giving them his name. He wanted them to have all the benefits of welfare. He lived with them and was a manager at his good job. Nightly he worked as a pimp, making more money than a lot of people.

Sadly, I've heard many more stories like this in my life. You people who live in the suburbs would have NO WAY OF KNOWING about this side of life. How could you? YOU WEREN'T THERE, *you never* LIVED *it*! My friends and I didn't move out of the city because "black" people moved in, we moved out because white people were/are being robbed, raped, beaten and even killed. If you have handicapped plates you're a target.

God to everyone: "I LOVE YOU! LOVE ME!!! That TYPE OF EVIL hate will keep YOU and YOURS OUT OF HEAVEN!!! GOD SEES ALL!!!!!

THE WORLD WILL NOT FIND PEACE UNTIL THIS WAR STOPS. Black and white makes grey."

God and Donna: "No one is hurting you but YOU! Learn English if you can. RESPECT *this country,* OUR *home."* A saying from the sixties, "America, love it or leave it."

Like a black comedian once said, "I don't know *why* we call ourselves *African Americans, I've BEEN to Africa and I am an* AMERICAN*!!!" What if a black person is NOT from Africa? While tourists were on safari in Africa, a hundred black terrorists,* came out of the woods looking for Americans to capture, rob, rape, and kill. (It just occurred to me that I typed that up above regarding some of the blacks in our cities. Is that what you want to pass down as your heritage?) Oprah canceled her plans to go on a safari. I FEEL Oprah and I through God, could heal black and white problems.

Donna: "Who's going to free *us*?"

God: "GOD!

Equality is for everyone. EVERYONE!!! Black, white, English and Irish, on and on, let's find the grey area. Whites and blacks, stop teaching your children this evil hate. Darker blacks, stop discriminating against lighter blacks and others. *Stop Satan's hate* NOW!!! NOW, *it's time for* EVERYONE *to get along. Stop it before it's too late for you and* YOUR *children*. Stop all the hate and deception NOW. Feel the love, *feel it, we love you. Please love me, too. Love yourselves, SAY*, 'I love myself!' Look in the mirror every day and say, 'I love myself,' 'I LOVE MYSELF!' "

Donna: "An older white man said to me, 'Look at the world today with all *these* interracial marriages.' The first thing that came to my mind was God saying to me, 'That's the way it *has* to be!' The second was, 'With *all* the problems this world is having with the ozone, rain forest, abuse and hate, *he* is worried about *that*?' Crazy. It is sad to think *that in order to love our neighbor*, we have to all be the same color; all have the same type eyes. Is that the only way to do it?" This was brought home to me when I was at a mall on St. Patrick's Day. An Irish band was playing, and standing next to me was a very Irish looking girl, who requested Danny Boy. She had three little children with her: one white, one mulatto and a small baby who was very dark. If that were thirty years ago, I don't think some of the people around her would have been so friendly. What a difference a day makes...O come ye back in *sunshine or in shadow*...Oh, Danny Boy, Oh Danny Boy, *I love you so*

. God: "If we all looked alike, would you find something else wrong with the people around you?

Yes, you would because *you're not happy with* YOU! Please *pray to be* WHOLE!!! When you get up in the morning, just be the BEST *person you* can be for that day! *Let's not blame anything on* ANYONE ELSE. Take responsibility for your own lives and yourselves. If I fail today, I have *no one* to blame but MYSELF! If you fail, *you fail on your own*. If you succeed, *you succeed on your own. I* can show you the road, but *only* YOU *can walk it*!"

God *bless you.*
God, I pray to be whole.

Chapter 22

Confusion Equals Satan

Donna: "What *is this* politically correct stuff?"

Donna and God: "I am who I am and if I am not trying to hurt you or life on this planet, *leave me alone*! I am responsible for me and you are responsible for you. If you don't like me, you don't like yourself. *We are all connected*, we *are* one. God *is us*. We have God *with us and around us*, we ARE *one*. The hero is YOU!"

Donna: "I usually just let spirit lead me, which keeps me in a safe, warm, happy, comfortable place. For some reason, both my new machines (stereo and tape recorder) stopped working, taking precious time away from the book. I felt I was close to completion and was happy about that. Evil around me was getting me VERY *frustrated, angry and* CONFUSED. God, you promised me protection."

God: "*I* am!"

Donna: "Why are my recorders not working?"

God: "You have to slow down."

Donna: "ALL I've learned. I feel like I've learned NOTHING."

God: "You have if you do not relax and take it a step at a time."

Donna: "Do I have to return my NEW *stereo* and buy another *tape recorder?* " (This one was only about a year old).

God: "No, they will work tomorrow. Trust me!"

Donna: "Time from that plane to this varies a little. In other words, you don't know if *it's tomorrow* or a *week from tomorrow. God had never said, 'Trust Me' to me before. I wonder why?* It's like a puzzle *where you don't have all the pieces*!?! Can't YOU just TELL *me* to slow down? Or *tell me* what's going on?"

God: "No. Don't just assume I will tell you everything. You have to see where I am coming from. As far as you go, is as far as I will be there for you. Don't lose the thought *I am* not, *you are*. Okay?" (I did not answer this because at first I did not understand it.)

Donna: "Some people are very lucky, *everything* goes their way. I feel like I have been swimming upstream all my life. What's up?" (I wrote this before the lesson about the weeds and the grass.)

God: "You have to be here to live your life. Don't look at the big picture."

Donna: "Which is?"

God: "You have to be here. Suffering is part of learning. You have to learn *more now* to go forward in life so you can rest up here. The book is not at rest yet, more needs to be put in."(A reminder: This was channeled *before* Chapter 2.)

Donna: "What else?"

God: "To put in some of your feelings of being unhappy and confused to show them you are human."

Donna: "I feel I am *more* human than others because of all my suffering."

God: "You are, you are but you are more holy also than a lot of people and they need to understand who *you*, Y-O-U are and where *you* are coming from."

Donna: "Thanks. What else?"

(?): zzzzzz' (3/29/99 Carol just said to me, "Oh, you don't know who said this" and these z's came up again.) "Go forward and see if there is a way to adopt into life to see if you can do the things that need to be done. Do it now or else I will send you to the other side to suffer the pains of *hell* on earth to see what it is like."

Donna: "Whenever confusion slips in, I always suspect Satan is here. Now I see how people can get angry with God when it was Satan all the time, not God, confusing their lives." (A bad feeling had come over me which I immediately got rid of with white light from God.)

Still Donna: "I don't believe GOD would say that to me or anyone else!"

(?): "He would if you don't do what he wanted."

Donna: "*This is a* LIE. HE said before, *he* would send me back with Adam and Eve to learn!?"

(?): "*He* will if you stop saying *no* to me."

Donna: "Who are you?"

(?): "Satan!"

Donna: "Why are you bothering me?" (Notice every time I *thought* negatively or bad or had anger, Satan slipped in. THAT'S how *easy* it is.)

God: "*Learn to* BE AWARE!!"

Satan: " 'Cause you are writing wrong."

Donna: "*You are a* LIAR!"

Satan: "YES!"

Donna: "Why do you come into children and hurt them? That's VERY WRONG."

Satan: " 'Cause we have to survive. Children are very easy to get into, especially when they are hurt, they get *angry* and call out for help. All you have to do is think of us as adults do and we are there to take you over. That's life in the big city."

Donna: "Leave my machinery alone so that I can get back to writing."

Satan: "No, you have to listen to my side. I have to live and die and survive. My life does *not* know about loving and listening to people who love life. We *hate* and *judge* and HATE *life as* it is. We like confusion and hate and we CREATE it."

Donna: "Why do you want people to know *that*? It will ruin your business."

Satan: "It is fair that they know we exist so that they can decide who to go with, you or me."

Donna: "That doesn't make sense to me."

Satan: "It will. People can have choices and choose to be evil. They are *stupid* enough to think they can *cheat* us/me *in the end.* They *can't! Let* THEM *know* THEY CAN'T!" (This was said to me VERY firmly.)

Donna: "That almost makes sense. I know people whom I have *told*, 'You are EVIL!' They don't want to believe it or don't want to face it or just don't care. I also know people that do whatever they want in life because they will ask for forgiveness at the last minute and once in heaven are at the bottom of the ladder. Also there are some who don't believe in *life after death* and that your SOUL *lives on.* Imagine the expression on their faces AFTER *their* BODY *dies*! They must like to *gamble*. Is that you in them confusing them?"

Satan: "Yes. They are open to doing bad things. It's easier than doing *good* things, *to us*."

Donna: "It is easier for you, not me. I don't like the bad feeling and negative feelings and sadness and loneliness that comes with you."

Satan: "We are *happiest when you are sad and lonely*!"

Donna: "That makes such sense and reminds me of an ex-boyfriend. I am open to being fair, but not to subject you to my life. *Go away* and *leave me* and *leave my friends alone*, and *everyone* who will *not* allow you in. SO BE IT . . . .SO IT IS!"

Donna still: "I think it is simplistic to say, 'When you are happy, that's God-like. When you are sad, that is Satan.' Like saying, 'The devil made me do it!' And the cartoons when you were a child, with Satan looking over your left shoulder (trying to make you do wrong) and the angel, looking over your right shoulder, telling you *that* is wrong and *showing you* how to do right. Please listen to your *Angel and deny* Satan. When Satan gives you lemons in life, ask God to make lemonade."

God: "Yes, Satan *is* that close to you. That's how easy he can *walk* into you. If you THINK something evil or negative (even if you want to steal something that cost only one dollar), you OPEN THE DOOR for him to come in."

Donna: "When I spoke to Dameon, I had to listen very hard to see if his voice would change, and you could hear, sometimes, just having a general conversation, an attitude coming in. He would go from nice, acting God like, back to insolent, overbearing, pompous and arrogant, Satan. So it is the voice, *a little,* but it is mainly WHAT HE SAYS and HOW HE SAYS IT. Once in a while, *I can see* a change flash across his *eyes* and I also see it in other people. It's Satan in them!"

God: "LOOK FOR IT and remember he is waiting every minute of the day and night to get *into* your body and soul to live there. Pray you don't die with him in you or YOU will go to his house of fire and hell *forever*. Satan is self-doubt and hate, despair, ego, stubbornness, jealously, etc., also a *con* man, a *con* woman, and *a liar*. If your child or relative is nice one minute and killing things the next, THAT'S Satan. Satan *does* go to church in human beings *for show* and sometimes they THINK they can *buy* their way into heaven. If you have hate, *he is you."*

Donna: "I was in my car and was cut off, that usually pushes *me* over the edge. I had *a lot* of anger and what came to me as clear as a bell was, 'If you don't like him, you don't like you.' I *instantly* calmed down."

God: "Satan uses anything he can to *try* to get you. He will tell you he spoke to a relative, friend or pet that has passed over to the other side and then give you a message from them to do something wrong, no matter how *small* it seems. If it doesn't seem *right* to you, *don't do it*! This is NOT to be confused with loving *God-like spiritualist*s who give you messages to help you better yourself in this life. Listen to *your Angel*. If it's something positive, GOOD, you can do it. If it is negative, BAD, *don't do it*!"

Donna: "For instance, Dameon/Satan called me. I had not spoken to him for a while and something told me to not tell him I had put my cat named YoYo, to sleep. The first thing out of his mouth was, 'Where's YoYo?' I said, 'Here. Why?' "

He would not tell me for a while (games), then said, "I had the strangest dream that she was sitting by my window sill washing her left leg." (That's the leg the needle went into to put her to sleep. It had given her a *great deal* of pain and made me VERY *sad*.)

He went on to say, "She seemed *very happy* and *content*. It was like she was real. I went over and touched the spot where she had been sitting and looked for fur. YoYo gave me a message for you. She wants you to be nicer to me."

All of a sudden an angry voice came *pouring* out of me, "WHAT DO YOU TAKE ME FOR, A FOOL?"

Donna and God: "Say this very firmly NOW, with *no* kidding around and in all sincerity in a VERY STRONG voice, like *you* KNOW who you are and you REALLY *mean this*.

'I am receptive *only* to the BEST *guidance*,
and the MOST HELPFUL *influences*!'

Say that *three times* and MEAN IT. And also in the same *strong, powerful voice* say three times:

'I am surrounded by a cloud of GOD'S *white light*
and PROTECTED from ALL *harm*!'

Although the sources of these are unknown, I have often heard our Reverend Doctor Erle Myers say them.

Say these or your own prayers of protection, as much as you can during the day, or at least once before you get out of bed and once before you go to sleep. Don't forget the *Our Father* and *Hail Mary*!!! Pray to Saint Michael for protection from evil and nightmares, which are also from evil Satan.

When you pass over, *if* you see the black hole and fires of hell, filled with evil-looking and evil-acting people, immediately pray to God and you will be saved. Your soul will go to God's land, but you will not be as close to God, as *you were* NOT close to God on this earth. You will have to learn your lessons from the very beginning, the BOTTOM of the ladder. Don't hurt people or animals in this life. *What goes around* DOES *come around, sometimes* a lot MORE than *three* times depending, on WHAT you did to someone or something and WHO you did it to, any living thing and objects are included. BELIEVE IT!!!"

Donna: "I was out buying a *new* tape recorder and I was tested three times this particular day, by Satan. A girl in the store, whom I had not seen for many years, had been leading a VERY *wild life*. She asked me if I would like to go for a drink. I declined. Then I got home and Dameon/Satan called me to see if I would go out with him. I did not. By now I was screening my calls, trying to figure out if there was the FULL

MOON, when I realized it was more lessons or rather testing. The phone rang once again. It was a guy I haven't been out with for a *long* time. He wanted me to go to a party. I respectfully declined. I pray for him all the time because he has a lot of confusion and illness in his life."

God: "He has to pray for himself."

God and Donna: "There were struggles. I haven't been out for a drink or to a party with liquor, for a long time. It was tempting to go out, leave the book and have a drink. After all, clean fun is not a sin. Singing, dancing and laughter, as a matter of fact, are very cleansing and healing for the soul & body. We all need to smile more. God, to sing and dance and laugh."

After I had refused all the drinks, I did feel *better* about myself. It was time for me to *go forward in a* DIFFERENT *way and direction* from all the drinking and partying which I have done in the past. I feel that I have passed the test. I am *finally learning* to pass tests.

After more than ten days without my tape recorder, I have obviously started taping the book again to give to a typist who thought listening to a tape would be faster than reading. The body of this book was actually written in seven days and nights. A year ago I was getting the book ready for print, the newer lessons were *almost* all interjected, and editing was almost all done. But who knew what God's plans were going to be for more stories and lessons? By the way, I returned the new tape recorder, the two machines started working properly again, as promised!

Chapter 23

Love, Respect, And Our Children

I saw an old black and white movie on TV last night, about a crook who dies. Someone comes for him and takes him to the other side, puts him in a room with all the liquor he can drink and a roulette table at which he *never* loses. The crook says, "I don't get it, I *thought* this place was only for school teachers and people like that."

A man, dressed in white, said, "Oh, we have *some* teachers here."

The crook said, "Well, there must have been some kind of mistake or something."

The man said, "Let's go look at your records of life." He takes out the crook's folder. "Well, at the age of five you stole from a store, at the age of six, you murdered a dog. At eight, you organized a gang and at fifteen, you killed a man."

The crook said to him, "I'm bored with this. I'm tired of just winning all the time now. I belong in the other place. Send me to the other place. I'll probably have more fun there. I don't want to be in heaven anymore."

The other man *laughing out loud* said, "What makes *you* THINK *you're in heaven*?" The devil then locked the crook in the room alone for eternity. It brings a whole new perspective to *working* HARD for what YOU *want* in life. RESPECT AND LOVE! Are YOU a gambling person? *Is there life after death?* The ball is in YOUR *court*!

***

I had to be strong for MYSELF *all* of my life. If I had to have an operation, I was on my own. Anything to do with school, I did with my friends, which was very nice. Family did not come. As a matter of fact, I needed a ride to my high school graduation. One brother drew the short straw, he started to drive me to my Junior High School. The only problem was, I was graduating from Hyde Park High School.

My mother and father never came to talent shows. They were more like my grandparents anyway. When I see an OLDER couple intentionally having children, I feel a *great deal* of SADNESS for THAT CHILD and also for all the *litters* of babies that are being born today because of science. Some doctors feel the same way and also feel that the doctors creating this should be prosecuted for endangering lives.

God: "There are a lot of BEAUTIFUL *older children* around that would LOVE a *good home*. *Selfishness*. LOVE *and* LEARN!"

Donna: "I have no regrets about NO *family* at my special occasions. It gave me more freedom to be *strong* and STAND on *my* OWN *two feet*. Some relatives try to put you in THEIR square box of EXPECTATIONS. Now I see that my freedom was in preparation for what I'm doing at this time in my life, to be able to put a roof over my head, all of my life, even though *I* LOST one roof through bankruptcy. I've learned the lessons of *knowing* where to go to get *your* INNER *strength*, and how to earn your own money, also to create prosperity through positive thinking. And if you don't know how, *you have to* LEARN *on your own*. No Mommy and Daddy, or Grandma and Grandpa to hand it over to you, because they're JUST NOT THERE."

God: "If the mother and father birds never made their babies leave the nest, they would *never learn to* FLY. Then what happens when the mother and father birds pass away? Teachers and parents make children LEADERS, *not* followers. At Christmas time, when your children all want the same dolls and sneakers, realize that someone gets paid a lot of money to brainwash you and your children, through commercials, to buy *their* products. What do we have to learn from this? Use your own head and feelings. What do YOU *really* want or *need*? BE YOUR OWN PERSON! STOP FOLLOWING LIKE SHEEP!"

Donna Marie: "If you're *not* the LEAD *dog*, the view NEVER changes. When we were children, we ALL wanted to be the king and queen of *the mountain*. We had very few toys so we *had* to use *our* IMAGINATIONS."

God: "I look around today and I just see children looking for and seeking a leader *in the streets* because *they don't have one in their homes.* Mothers and fathers *look in the* MIRROR."

God and Donna: "I overheard a woman say to her three year old, 'Do you want a nap?' "

As cranky as he was, he never took a nap, HE didn't want one. YOU'RE the ADULT, so ACT like the adult. This is what amazes me. Parents like her are going to be wondering, when their children are in their early teens and older, WHY they don't listen to them or show them respect. Then they will ask, "Why?" Then they will blame everyone *for miles around,* even their *children,* EVERYONE but THEMSELVES. EGO!

God: "That is a grey area. The children will have to take some responsibility for bringing THEMSELVES up as NICE *people,* RESPECTABLE *people* with good character."

Donna: "But how are they going to learn *that* on their own? I SAW respect for others from my family."

God: "The children of today will have to seek out SPIRITUAL *teachers* to help guide them."

Donna: "For instance, the 'Oprah Winfrey Show' teaches and shows people how to care for themselves and others. This is wonderful, but we all have to help and do our share to make it work. Is it enough? *Are you helping?"*

God and Donna: "As for the children who *do not* want to better themselves and *are a threat* to *good human beings,* get them *off* of the streets and *out* of the schools NOW, so other people and children can walk and learn in PEACE and SAFETY. Put these children of Satan into the service at *earlier* ages or jail, or let's create a service that will take them. Bring classroom and God's schooling there. Let them *learn* from someone else what DISCIPLINE is. Instead of closing our air force bases, use them to discipline children, as they do in a Texas 'Boot Camp.' Teach children from the first grade on up how to love and respect themselves, people and animals, etc. Teach them good manners. Bring back the Pledge of Allegiance and *prayer.* It would only take one determined person to do so. An atheist, who was called 'the most hated woman in America' fought to take prayer out of public schools. Train children all in CPR and basic animal emergency care. Make them required courses in high school and college."

God: "You have something to give. I expect something from you.

God and Donna: Good people, who have lost loved ones due to acts of hate from children, are now suing the parents of the children committing these awful crimes against society. You HAVE to change these hundred year old laws to *protect law abiding citizens. Instead of* protecting and setting men FREE who abuse their wives, or women who stalk men and get away with it. *Instead of* helping rapists, child molesters, people who abuse animals, drunk drivers, and gun carrying children, etc., to get out of jail, get together and change these laws. These laws are costing us too much money and *far too many* LIVES!! Also, *hold the news media accountable* for the problems THEY INTENTIONALLY CREATE, especially racial, for sensationalism creating more hate, havoc and news only to win awards and be competitive. DON'T SUPPORT THEM, call and cancel that newspaper, turn off that station, teach them a lesson they won't soon forget. Do it now before it's too late. Are there any lawyers, retirees or *anyone else* that would like to tackle that? LET'S DO IT NOW."

God: "You start *it* and WE will follow behind! I PROMISE YOU!"

Donna: "We believe and trust in YOU, 1-4-3."

God: "Thank ALL of your *teachers,* but if you fail, you fail alone. If you go to heaven, *you* have SUCCEEDED ON YOUR OWN."

Donna: "This has happened to me SO MANY times. I come out of a store and parked next to me is a truck or car with an animal locked in it. Whether it's winter or summer, it's not right. Once, there was a large, black dog in a truck on a VERY *hot, humid day,* panting away. People either don't care or just don't realize how easily and quickly (within 15 minutes) their pets, and children, could and do die. That also goes for people who take their dogs jogging. Bring some water for them, let them rest more or just *don't* bring them if you are going far or too fast. Use the BRAIN *God* gave you. They have fur coats to protect them from the cold and sunburn, but it's NOT *enough* for extreme cold (especially if they're in a warm house all day, they need sweaters like you do) and it's *too hot* to RUN *too far*. I know God put this dog next to my car for me to rescue. It was so hot, I really didn't feel like getting the person's plate number and make of the truck and walking *all* the way back to the store, but I did it. I did it because *it was the right thing to do*! *I* will be able to sleep better tonight. As I was taking down the information, a mother, father, grandmother and three children walked by, looked at the dog suffering, then *kept walking*."

Satan said "Don't do that good deed, forget about it, he'll be OK."

God and Donna: "*Wake up* people! What a wonderful lesson in compassion those children missed from YOU *adults*. They could have taught their children and they, theirs. *You* begin it now. YOU *don't wait for the next person*. Create good adults! Dog officers should also be responsible for rescuing dogs and other animals left in cars, etc., not just for dogs walking down the street alone. Hire CAT officers!

WE have *no* respect for people who leave children and/or animals in cars. WE are also VERY UPSET with people who leave their animals tied up outside all day and night. That annoying bark is trying to tell everyone something, come here, play with me, take me in and take care of me, feed me and give me water in clean bowls. It's a cry for help. Also, animals *do not belong in cage, especially dogs and cats*. Why do you have them? Why bother??? YOU are KILLING *them*. They need COMPANIONSHIP, too. Give your pet to a home that will treat them better and love them more. Don't make *them* suffer because YOU *do*. Call the humane societies on those people today. If there's no law in your town, MAKE ONE. Be prepared for disasters. They have to have clean water, food, respect, exercise, a warm home, groomed, vet appointments, licenses and love. And RESPECT your neighbors. God *is* watching. Do that good deed. Don't forget about it – They won't be Okay!!!

I am richer, happier and healthier every day, in every way!

For a few years in a row, I took my girlfriend's daughter out to a place of her choice, a couple of weeks after her birthday. This year she, Mary, turned seven, going on THIRTY-seven. After we had lunch, we went to the home of a friend, who has a pool and children around Mary's age. When she became bored there (after ten minutes), she asked me, "Can we stop at your apartment? I want to see your cats. Do you still have the black and white one, Bartet?"

I said, "Yes, I do."

She asked, "What does Bartet mean anyway?"

I replied, "Bartet is also known as Bas, Bast or Bast-et. She is the goddess of ancient Egypt having the body of a woman and the head of either a lion or a cat."

"How did you get Bartet?" she asked.

I replied, "A couple of years ago, I was the manager and rental agent for a few buildings. Not only did I let cats into the building, even though they were not allowed, I rescued strays, brought the kittens or cats to the vet's and then gave them to the tenants in these buildings making sure the tenants followed up at the vet's. One day, I was in my office during Hurricane Bob, a black and white cat suddenly ran by my window soaking wet. The poor thing was so wet her tail was as skinny as a pencil. The day before I had noticed her under a bush *not* succeeding at catching birds." I thought, "Oh, God, let me help that poor cat." Within a couple of days, she was crying VERY loudly at our side door. I ran and got our maintenance man who quickly picked her up and took her to his office. She had been in a fight and had a little cut under her neck. The maintenance man said she was born under the dumpster out back about a year ago. He had been feeding her every day. She was SO *friendly* NO ONE believed she was a homeless cat. I couldn't have another cat where I lived at that time because the landlady didn't like cats and I already had two cats, YoYo who was fourteen and my Tabby who was fifteen years old. Tabby had been a stray whom my good friend Rainie brought to my door many years ago, and said to the tiny, adorable, tabby ball of fur, "Meet your new mother!" I got my beautiful Siamese cat, named YoYo, who had also been abandoned, to keep Tabby company. They would not have been thrilled to see Bartet. But SHE had other ideas. I took her to the vet's, and Althea Griffin from her Humane Society paid most of the bill. Thank heavens for Althea, her sister Muriel and the other helpers who also volunteer their valuable time! Then I tried desperately to find Bartet a good home, as I had, *more easily,* for a lot of other homeless cats. I would stop by the maintenance man's office to say, "Hi!" to the cat. If there were five other people petting her she would leave them and come running to me.

The people would say, "SHE IS YOURS!"

I said, "I can't have three cats! But so much for what *I* want, not to mention *my* landlady, who might as well have been 'Dameon's' mother. I took Bartet home and she immediately went over to where my cats were eating, put her head under theirs, PUSHED their heads up out of *their* cat bowls and started eating their food, what's even MORE amazing was, *they* LET HER *do it*!!!"

The landlady came in when I wasn't home *pretending* something was broken. She counted the three dishes, then called me and said, "You have to get rid of your three cats."

I said, "I'll move out!" Because I was a good tenant, who paid early and kept her condo cleaner than it ever was before, she quickly changed her mind. I felt as if I couldn't breathe living there. I couldn't even hang up a picture. Landlords are missing a lot of great tenants by not accepting "fixed" cats into their dwellings.

A few months earlier, a neighbor had brought his cat up to visit and both my cats cornered it, yet they accepted the stray which I brought home.

Mary said, "I think God made it so Bartet wanted you first, then God made it so that you wanted her so that you could be together."

After that story she wanted to know if Tabby and YoYo, were there. I told her, "No, Tabby didn't live much past fifteen. Yo Yo became heart broken (so did I), then her health slowly deteriorated. She was almost nineteen years old, when she became very sick, and I had to have her also humanely put to sleep. *I miss her* SO *much,* I wanted HER back again." I was in town at the same shelter where I had gotten the three kittens before, I was bringing some things to their yard sale. While looking at all the cats I looked straight ahead and saw "my" Tabby staring back at me, he was frantically trying to get free to get to me, he swung at his brother (as if to say leave me alone) who was looking at him wide eyed and bewildered. Tabby had been dead for about two years. I was crying so hard I could not see straight, I ran back to Diane and asked how old he was? She answered, "About two years old." I was with a guy who JUST wanted to go to dinner but I told him to take me home instead. I, like Tabby, just wanted to be left alone. At home I called Diane and left a couple of messages to call me as soon as possible. Then I prayed, should I take Tabby and his brother who looked almost identical to him, keeping in mind I almost got evicted because of *three* cats. I said to God, "If they are gone when I call back I will know that it wasn't meant to be." I called the next day *again* and this time Diane answered and said they were adopted by a couple who own a big house and are never having children. I was still hurt and devastated. She would not give me their phone number nor them mine. I still miss him, and I'm sorry I didn't just grab him and take him home again. That's why I was looking for "my" cat, YoYo. I have called again for information about Tabby, but Diane moved out of state. If you or someone you know adopted two male tabby cats around "1993" from the Ellen Gifford Animal Shelter in Boston please get in touch with me. I only want to see him and touch him once more.

Getting back to Mary: Mary hesitated then said, "I think God is making *one* for you right now up in heaven and I am going to say a prayer to God that *your* cat comes back to you and that she is born close enough for you to find her." At that point I was holding back the tears.

When I dropped Mary off, she said, "Don't come to my party next year, so we can go out again all day for my birthday present." That's a good deal. That's the nicest invitation to *not* go someplace I have ever received. It's very grounding to hang around with children, isn't it? I am not used to being around someone with such an honest trust in God. Even though I know a lot of people who STUDY *the Bible*, go to church every week and read every book on spiritualism they can get their hands on, *she's* LIVING IT and BELIEVING IT!! We need to be more childlike to be *that close* to God. Please help the homeless children and cats and pray for government funding. Thank you!!!

An acquaintance, named Barbara, brought her seven year-old daughter to church one day. At one point in the sermon, the Reverend said, "Is there anyone else we should pray for?"

The little girl raised her hand, "Could we please pray for my grandmother? She is going to go to heaven soon."

The Reverend said, "HEAVEN! What *a* WONDERFUL *place! We are* ALL going *to heaven* some day!"

The girl quickly responded, "*Ohhh, NO, she's* making THIS *trip* ALONE!!!"

We need to be more childlike to be that close to God!

Chapter 24

The Well Is Never Dry

July 1995: on a Sunday about a year ago, I was watching "Picket Fences." This was the show in which the two boys put a live frog in the freezer. They stood there, describing all the noises it was making as it died. What an awful message to give kids. Who cares if the frog was *still really* in the freezer or not. Anyway, frogs have survived millions of years before WE came along. The day they dissected frogs in school I stayed home, with my mother's permission. Now those we have left are being born deformed. Our future?! I was becoming physically sick, so I turned off the show and *never* watched it again. It stuck with me for over a week (remember I said don't hide behind curtains anymore).

Well, I really felt I *had to* write a letter telling the network how I felt. (Believe it or not, I really hated to write.) About halfway through the letter, a message came through from God, *very clearly,* which I could not deny. God said to them, "You will win no more awards! You *will win no more awards*!"

Well, I never watch the awards or beauty pageants. They bore me to tears. *Except for the Genesis Awards*, which should be advertised more, are given to the people and stars who help all animals. Thank Heavens for people like you. Keep up the GOOD work.

The next day, "coincidentally," I learned "Picket Fences" had won awards two years in a row. My left brain said to my soul, "God, that's a far reach that they won't win even one award in 1995, but I *felt* that it was true."

This week I learned, surprise, surprise, NO nominations, NOT ONE! You will win NO awards this year. Coincidence!

God To The People: "Don't test me!"

Donna: "By the way, I just found a copy of the letter I mailed to them. It's a miracle I could find it so fast. I have a file cabinet FILLED with papers and not very organized. I opened a drawer and put my hand *right on it. I was shaken.* The letter was dated September 21, 1994, the show was aired on August 26th. The second paragraph said, 'The children were never even punished, you will win NO AWARDS next year.' "

The show was actually canceled not long after that.

God: "Don't be afraid to step from behind the curtain and help. *You* CAN make a difference."

Donna: "I know in my heart now, that none of my machines worked so I could learn these new lessons and share them with you. The well *is* never dry!"

Chapter 25

God's Creatures

God, this book has been a hardship. And *now* my apartment has bugs, with stingers, crawling on my couch. I haven't seen those since I lived on Norwell Street many years ago. I was on the third (top) floor, five room, two-bedroom apartment with six other people, one female cat, who looked like Angel, and a lot *less* bugs. (I guess there was no room for them.) Now I'm next to the water, living on the third (top) floor in a two bedroom apartment. I have two female cats and a lot of bugs (never a cockroach). Go figure! More circles.

Donna: "Will it never end?"

God: "Yes."

Donna: "When?"

God: "Now."

Donna: "God, enough is enough. God, *enough is enough.* God, *enough is ENOUGH.* How could you forsake me?"

God: "I don't know. *YOU* have the ability to stop it."

Donna: "How? *Please.*"

God: "Sell yourself to the universe and say, '*Don't let anyone or anything get to you.*' And say it in a *FIRM way.*"

Donna: "Where are all these bugs coming from? And how do I get rid of them?"

God: "Say, 'I won't accept them, GO AWAY NOW. I command you *IN THE NAME OF GOD*!!' "

Donna: "Thank you."

The more sensitive I become, children, animals, birds, and even bugs come to me now. I had a little spider come in through the window. I looked at it as just *another bug* to get rid of, then the second it came to my mind to let him stay and get rid of the other bugs for me, it stopped running from me and instantly started making its nest. I have learned a lot from that little spider, which almost scares me because spiders are *not* my favorite thing to have around. Now I go in and look at him. Did you catch anything today? He *knows* he's safe, it's *almost* as if he's another pet. My cats have not even bothered him.

A huge fly came in today. I don't know *where* he came from. I chased him for ten minutes, then I finally said, "Well, I have a little spider that could probably eat you for about three weeks." He quickly flew to the sliding doors, I opened it and he swiftly left. It was a nice arrangement after all. I'm learning to live more in harmony with the universe, not that I want my home over run with bugs. *I do not.* But the bug sprays are killing *us* and our pets, NOT just the bugs. Instead, I now put a jar over the bugs – they go to the bottom of it, I put a cover over it and then put them out – it's easier, safer, cheaper and there's no MESS. It's less traumatic for me and for the bugs when I use the jar. I used to hate chasing them around the house and watch them slowly suffocate from the spray and eventually die. In gardens without pesticides, the birds eat the caterpillars. The food is healthier and you do need to plant a little more to SHARE with the animals.

God: "The bugs are smarter than people."

Donna: "Some bugs actually adjust to the poisons. WE *do not,* and our pets *do not,* and our waters *do not.* We and our pets become MORE sensitive to the poisons. Just a thought!

To the evil people who try to run over an animal who's only ambition is to cross the street."

God: "This is where *they* belong, not *you, evil*!!!"

The little bird on the balcony: Chirp, chirp, help us, *help us now, we are dying.*

Where I used to live, I saw a crow knock a duck off of her egg and eat it, as she looked on helplessly as I was forced to do because I live on the fourth floor. It was sad. I don't ever want to see anything like that again. There HAS to be a way to *stop the crows* from eating the eggs of the other birds before it's too late. There's a small town in New York which has 50,000 crows gathering each year. No one knows why they gather there. They will try to get them to move on by playing the sound of crows in distress. They might need to take more desperate measures. The birds *are* HERE !!!

A large company in Cincinnati still kills rabbits, using them for testing, pouring poison on their bodies and in their eyes. You cannot get accurate results with all these huge people holding down this tiny rabbit, abusing it. Imagine the stress factor of an animal cowering in the corner of a cage seeking protection to no avail. You can imagine how inaccurate these tests must be, holding down this little five pound animal, to inject it with poisons *until it slowly dies*. There are other ways. Remember when you used to have to kill a rabbit to find out if you were pregnant? Now there is a little test that takes you one minute. No animals have to be killed or tested on. Thank you, God!

There are still some laboratories who violate the Animal Welfare Act while conducting tests on animals. They experiment on all types of animals, taking organs out of them and leaving them to bleed to death with no pain medication or anesthesia. I am telling you, so you will do something about it. There is much more going on. I will spare you from the rest of the *horror* stories. If I thought it would push you over the edge to help them, I would tell you. But I'm going to pray that you will be concerned enough to make that call or write that letter to say you don't like what's going on. Stop buying their products. Call them. Ask if they still test on any animals. People for the Ethical Treatment of Animals (PETA) will send you their "Do and Don't Test" list of companies, as well as a list of health charities that are cruelty-free if you call them at 757-622-7382. Ever since I've been using creams and makeup with only natural herbs and vitamins in them, which I purchased from a health food store, everyone has been telling me my skin looks beautiful and I look younger. Naturally, none of these products have chemicals in them and are never tested on animals.

The law demands that humans used as test subjects for new drugs, be given ALL information regarding side effects and potential risks so we can make an informed choice. Animal tests are not a good indication of how a drug will perform in humans. Humans are test subjects for all new drugs that have been tested on animals. Animal tests are not a good indication of how a drug will perform in humans. Ironically, unfavorable animal test results do not prevent a drug from being marketed for human use. So much evidence has accumulated about differences in the effects that chemicals have on animals and humans that government officials often do not act on findings from animal studies. In the last two decades, many drugs were taken off the market after causing hundreds of deaths and/or injuries. In fact, more than half the drugs the FDA approved between 1975 and 1985 were either removed from the market or re-labeled because of serious side effects. If the pharmaceutical industry switched FROM *animal experiments* TO quantum pharmacology and in vitro tests, WE would have *greater protection*, not less. Animals do not have that choice. A person would not choose to be locked in a cage for seven days a week without seeing the light of day or having a choice of what food is thrown at him, or what needle, pill, or operation he's to receive.

Have you read the warning on the back of your tube of toothpaste? Mine reads: "Keep out of reach of children under six years of age. If you accidentally swallow more than used for brushing, seek professional assistance or contact a *poison* control center immediately." Can you believe that? I called the 800 number listed on the back to ask what ingredient was poisonous. She answered, "Fluoride." I was surprised when she said, "Fluoride", because I thought it would be Sodium Lauryl Sulfate (SLS), another ingredient in our shampoos and toothpaste (and God knows what else). I told her I heard on a radio station that it caused brain damage in children among other things. She said she'd get back to me. She never did of course. They also test this on animals. In the old days they used Baking Soda to clean their teeth. If they accidentally swallowed too much, it would cure a stomach ache and other things, rather than harm you, your children or any animals.

The protective helmets you are wearing were tested by strapping them on monkeys and *dropping them on their heads*. Did you know that? And car manufacturers, even though they had dummies, use to put dogs in the back seats to see what kind of injuries would occur. Happily they no longer use animals in crash tests. If you work in a laboratory and have witnessed or have evidence of animal cruelty, PETA offers a reward of $500.00 dollars *or more* for information, photographs, or videotape leading to exposure of and sanctions against a laboratory. PETA guarantees absolute confidentiality. You may reach them at 757-622-7382. You don't have to use your name, please call now. Thanks PETA for editing the animal sections of this book! While other countries and religions honor and live in harmony with the cat and feed them, there are some people overseas and in the United States who are keeping them in very small cages and eating them. They also eat dogs and squirrels. People are complaining their pets are disappearing. Unfortunately they are more often stolen to be used in laboratories. If you overhear someone talking about it, turn them in. If you made a mistake (which I doubt you will do), that's okay, too. At least *you* tried and you will be able to sleep better at night. How could a big, huge person look down at this little animal, look into their eyes, their souls, and still eat them.? *Where are their souls?* Where are they? Who could look at such a helpless animal and kill them in an appalling cruel way? What type of an "animal" must you be to do that? Why do we call some animals *pets* and some *dinner*??

God: "Stop, whether it's for money or not, stop it now, stop it yesterday. And love! Send that letter in, you can do it. Make *them* aware that you're aware!"

Donna: "Make them put in their commercials that *they don't test on animals* and *prove it to us*. Then, only buy those products which they don't test on animals! Let them know how you feel. I won't stand for it anymore, will you?" "Disinfectants slowly kill your pets. If you have allergies, runny nose, etc., be aware of the warning on your products. In reading a label on a can of disinfectant at the top in large print it says: 'Spray around pet areas and household areas.' In *tiny* print at the bottom of the same can it says, 'Precautionary statement: *Hazardous to humans and domestic animals. Do not spray in eyes, on skin or clothing. If it gets in your eyes flush with water for fifteen minutes.' EPA registered for use in hospitals. Note to physicians: Measures against respiratory depression, circulatory shock and convulsions may be needed. Remove all contaminated clothing before reuse of disinfectant."* Tea tree is a REAL plant that disinfects naturally and obviously does not harm you if you get any on you, your pets or children. Also on their label is the notation: "Buyer assumes risks of handling and use." The good news is: Your home MIGHT smell better for a couple of seconds. The bad news is: You, your pets and children could become severely ill. I described the notation to a police officer. He said, "That's assault with intent." Don't we pay someone in the government to read our labels to protect us?

We spray it in pet areas, they walk in it and then wash it off of their paws with their tongues. Then your pet gets sick and you must bring it to the vet's. That's a whole other story. "I don't know what's wrong," the vet says. "Give him all this expensive medicine and come back and give me more money." Then there's another hundred dollars here and there. Vets will *have* to be accountable for what they do and *don't* do for our animals behind closed doors, especially during operations. Some sneaky vets charge you for the anesthesia and only give your pet a little inexpensive (for him) pill to knock your pet out for a *short* time while he operates. This cruelty could be happening in *your* neighborhood. It's happening in mine. Why couldn't it happen in yours? There's a vet in Boston who quotes one price over the phone and then when you're in his office and most vulnerable, the price has gone up three-fold. Yes, it's *against the law*. I wrote a letter with all of the facts and sent a copy to the appropriate board. The vet didn't make me pay the bill.

Read ALL your labels, then RUN don't walk to your nearest store which sells products that are all natural, not tested on animals, and *are* safe for us, our children and our pets.

God: *"Veterinarians, we* are watching *you now*!"

Donna: "I know how painful it is when you *must* have your pet humanely put to sleep. I have *had* to do it twice in the past two years. *Go* into the room at the vet's with your pet.

They deserve *at least that* much *from you*. Make sure it's done right away. Make sure it's done painlessly. Make sure it's done. We have a vet in a nice suburb who was *not* doing what he promised and was supposed to be doing. *One* thing I will tell you he did *not* do, was send the animals to the pet cemetery which people had chosen and paid extra for. Instead, he pocketed the money and sent the bodies of their pets to the local dump."

God: *"We are watching you."*

Donna: "It's difficult getting help to catch him. I needed money to hire private detectives. The smaller humane societies were rightly afraid of a counter-suit. When I could find no help, I called the Humane Society of the United States. They sent me an application for a *donation*, which was ironic because I had just told them I had gone bankrupt. I guess the millions *they* have is just not enough for all the animals. The smaller humane societies are willing to donate their time and a lot of times their *own* money to rescue the animals. In my will, I have left money to the small humane society which has helped me all of these years."

God: "Remember them in *your* will."

Donna: "Today the humane society will no longer come to get a cat out of a tree. Sometimes, firemen who love animals will do it on their own time."

God: "Thank you!"

***

One afternoon I was drawn to the small mall at the end of my street. Once there I felt the need to sit and relax for awhile, so I stopped in at a restaurant in the mall. While sitting at the bar eating a snack and reading the paper, I couldn't help wondering, "Why am I *really* here?" It was almost like "from my thoughts to God's ears," because one of the two other people in the place, was talking about how he thought his cat, who had a litter of kittens who were only a few month old, might be pregnant again. I said, "I'll help you. I help people with unwanted pets all the time and I'm looking for a special kitten to replace my Siamese cat who passed away around Mother's Day in May."

He introduced himself as Mark and replied, "That's strange, my cat is Siamese and her kittens were born around May."

Excitedly I asked, "How soon can I see them?"

He said, "As soon as you'd like. I'll call you." He didn't call me for a *couple* of weeks.

When he finally did call, on Tuesday I didn't feel comfortable going alone, so I took along a girlfriend to see the kittens. One little, black kitten, even though it was scared and wild, let me pick it up. A black cat was the last thing I wanted. I was looking for one that looked like my Siamese. Remember? They really do pick us don't they? I told him I wanted to take this one home, figuring I would give him to a nice home.

He said, "No. I promised that one to someone else." I felt that was not true, after asking again, I gave up. We could not get near the other two kittens because they were hiding in the cellar except for one cute, wild tiger kitten who was surprisingly perched on top of the couch staring over at me. Mark swooped her up and started to hand her to me while saying, "This is the one I thought was for you." But she looked like my Tabby cat except with short fur, not like YoYo, so I panicked and said, "There are A LOT of cats I could adopt, but I'm looking for a *special ONE*." I think that little kitten felt that rejection because she had a deep knowing look in her eyes (soul) like she knew something I didn't. That look turned quickly to sadness when I rejected her.

In the car my friend said, "Mark had honest eyes and seemed like a nice guy."

The next day I started setting up appointments for four kittens and the mother cat at the vet's. I also made many calls looking for room at *no-kill* shelters. It took me about three days, because as usual, all the shelters were filled. Two small organizations that volunteer their time, were willing to pay for everything because they felt it was an unsafe situation for the kittens, as they were living wild in a flea-infested cellar. I called Mark to tell him I would pick up the kittens and take them to my home. I was going to tame them for their new homes by leaving them alone until they trusted me enough to come to me. I called Saturday, but he didn't pick up the phone. I got a bad feeling so I said into his answering machine, "I'm *on my way*, anyway."

He called me right back to say, "They're *gone*." They got out, they are gone! I'll come and help you look for them! No, there's no use there gone!! Well, after all I've learned, I still lost it! After many hours of effort on my part and the humane society's part, and hundreds of dollars put aside for *his* cats, (even though the vet was giving a thirty percent discount) he thought I would just DROP it! I *really* lost it. I am not proud of it. What a test. I flunked. Perhaps not totally, because as I drove *by* his house, something told me "don't go in." I might have ended up in jail. I called him again but he *would not* let me come down to help him look for the kittens. (He was obviously NOT looking.) I said, "I'm not playing anymore games with you. You have a choice, either me or the M.S.P.C.A will come to look for the kittens and the cat. (They still go out for abuse cases, certain employees who answer say, "Our hands are tied," You have to *convince some of* THEM. A girl who answered on another day was VERY helpful. Unfortunately they're too busy with many cases.) I left it in the hands of the humane societies, the M.S.P.C.A., and God. I *started* to calm down but the stakes were the lives of his pets, and that was too high for me. I had been *too* nice to him for a month. I felt he took advantage of that. Maybe if I had been more firm sooner, he would have done the right thing. Or he might have become defensive sooner. I can't second guess! But I want a balance in my life *now.*

God: "Don't let him tell you what to do. Even though they are *his* cats, there is abuse. You have a right to help them *and you will!"*

Donna: "Well I received that message from God on Sunday."

When I called two rescue leagues, I got a recorded messages on Saturday AND Sunday, so for now, my hands were tied. I got in my car and drove to his house on Sunday. I couldn't sleep the night before so I *had* to do something. I spoke to six of his neighbors, the woman who lived right behind him said he had a lot of parties. No one had seen *any* kittens. I left my card and a lot of hope behind. At the risk of being seen, I walked into his yard. The little handmade cat door in the cellar window, *was closed.* He told me he always left it open because the mother cat drove him crazy crying to be let out. I think that statement was *too true*!

Later, when I told the girl who had originally come with me, he wouldn't let me help him look for the kittens, she said that he probably killed them and that she was a poor judge of character. Thanks, I wasn't upset enough. That's a *lesson* for *all* of us!

Getting back to Sunday, I was on the last page of this book when all this happened. At first I thought, "Something keeps preventing me from finishing. Why?" But I had to put the book aside again.

Monday I finally called the vet, Mark had not canceled the mother cat's appointment to be neutered on the following Thursday. The two humane societies said, "Call and turn him in." So I called again. The M.S.P.C.A.'s line was *busy. Sad.* When I finally got through, they said (after some convincing from me) that they would go to his house and ask to see his cat and kittens. If Mark wasn't home, they would go to where he works. They have the same rights as the police do. The laws have to be updated to protect the *animals, not* the abuser. Aren't we carrying the Constitution just a little too far?! Add an amendment to the Constitution to protect the trees, animals, children, elderly, the retarded and innocent people in a *very strict* manner.

Monday at 5:30 P.M. Mark called me, "Did you call the M.S.P.C.A. on me?"

Donna: "Yes!"

Mark: "Why did you do that?"

Donna: *"I told you Saturday, I was going to* if you wouldn't let me help you find the kittens."

Mark: "They were hiding under the cellar stairs."

Donna: "Why didn't you call me?"

He started swearing at me. I hung up on him. He called me back two times swearing. I hung up.

The third time he said, "All right I won't yell at you anymore. He went on to say, I was angry because a lot of people were yelling at me and using me."

Donna: "So *you* decided to *yell at me*."

Mark: "Yes. The kittens are gone again."

Donna: "Mark, look up and tell me what color the sky is in your world."

Mark, after a little silence: "I have *one* of them."

Donna: "Can I come down and get it?"

Mark: "Yes."

I was in a dress ready to go to a Monday night spiritual service. I drove to his house as fast as I could.

When I got there, ironically he handed me the *same tabby* kitten which he tried to give me before. (Spirit was really working overtime to get me this little angel.)

He angrily said, "I HAVE *all four.*" We had to chase the other three around the cellar before we finally captured them. Then, because they were old enough, we bathed them quickly in flea baths. (Which didn't help, we didn't comb them, they were *too* WILD! I wish I had the organic flea treatment).

He said, "Sorry for yelling at you and thanks for all the help."

Donna: "Okay."

After two calls to him on Thursday, he brought his cat in to be fixed. She wasn't pregnant and had no AIDS or feline leukemia which isn't contagious to people. The kittens are fine to sell to *nice* homes. These homes will have them *neutered* when they're about six months old, so we can stop this AWFUL *overpopulation problem.* One reason the humane organization has to sell them is they have already had all their kitten shots and some pay for half the neuter operation, IF they have enough money.

The reminder from God came to me again: "You have a right to help them *and you will.*"

Donna: "Thanks for everything, God. Thanks to the M.S.P.C.A., great job. All they had to do was show up, and it worked."

The other organization never called me back. Is it true that top executives get six figure salaries plus new expensive cars? If all this is true we could use that money, to buy a couple of new vans every year and hire more honest and loving people, to help the cats and kittens just as we had done.

God: "Help the people! Thanks to the people at the animal organizations who earn little or no money and give their whole hearts and souls."

Donna: "If some of the larger organizations *do* pick up a cat, it's usually just to put it to sleep. *Have your pet neutered* or *don't have a pet*!" There *are* some smaller organizations who will pay part of the vet bill, and in some cases all of the bill. Don't let *your fear* prevent you from bringing your pet to the vet. It's better for the pet to be fixed than to have unwanted young ones. Don't be selfish because YOU want the animal to have kittens or puppies! Thanks Bob Barker for using your show to help the animals!

One woman said to me, "But the animal will be so afraid." That's *her* fear and laziness speaking. When the pet comes home, he/she will be happier and a more loving pet. Your pet *is* worth a few calls and the little love that you will be showing him/her, after *all they* do for you. They do more than you realize, *believe me*.

Please do not put a flea collar on your animal after a flea bath. My girlfriend's cat died that way, next to her bed. There are other ways today to get rid of fleas. I was telling Althea how I missed church because I was rescuing the kittens.

She said, "That's all right. You're going to heaven!"

God: "So is she and all the *unselfish* people like her...the *unsung heroes*, the *true saints here on this earth*!"

The shelter just called me to tell me they now have room for all four of my kittens. I am sad again, but I am going to *learn my lesson* and *be resilient*!!! God, please give me the strength I need to give them over to the shelter, then I brought all four in. This is probably just how Mark felt, in his own way, about giving up the kittens.

God: "Except *now* they have been to the vet's and are in a room with wall-to-wall carpet, all sorts of toys, blankets and food. A more *showing* way *of love* than *just* feeling, *and hiding* and *too* painful for *him* to *let go* even though *it's better for them. Love. I love you, love me!!!"*

1/99: Like my dead plant.

Foster parents and others who have had to give up someone or something they love to give them a better life, truly know *unconditional love*!!! I've been praying to fill the empty space that YoYo left, when an answer came to me, "None of these kittens are for you." That doesn't feel right to me. What's going on? I've had many cats cross my path in the past few months and none are for me? I'm beginning to see that Satan doesn't want me to be happy or get my way. The more happy you are, the more power you have. I mean *truly happy*! On my way *back* to the shelter, the name *Angel* was coming to me again. The other three kittens were ignoring me, even the black male kitten that had initially come to me at Mark's house. *I* picked up the *tabby* kitten. Mark had intentionally handed to me twice, who was again staring at me, and I kept her...*Angel. (Later I got Angel a black cat to keep her company. I named him Ramses.)*

After I got home from the shelter with Angel, I remembered a dream I had the night before that this one, out of the four, had been adopted by someone else and died. As it turned out she had an infection that someone else might not have noticed because she was crying a little in the litter box. I had to bring her to a couple of vets because the first vet cost me a fortune and put Angel and myself through a great deal of stress with his misdiagnosis. He should have refunded my money. Is there malpractice for vets? Please *insist* on your vet giving *pain pills* for our pets after they have been operated on, or ANY painful treatment. Just because they *can't speak* doesn't mean they aren't IN *pain*. They can send a man to the moon and UFO's can land (Ezekiel 1:15), take us up and experiment on us, but they can't create a tiny pain pill, for a *billion* dollar a year industry, which is for our LOVING *HELPLESS* pets.

It just took me three days of playing with a string and then leaving Angel alone (I did pet her a little a couple of times to get my scent on her) for her to *start* being friendly and going up to my other cat, Bartet. The funny thing is, I got a cat who reminds me of both YoYo and Tabby. By the way, little Mary gave me a wonderful present from our day together. My kitten, Angel, was born just after Mary's birthday. Angel was living in a cellar only about three miles from my home. The owner of the mother cat, Mark, who had shown me his pendant of Mother Mary had said to me," This one's for you," as he handed me Angel. I looked down at Angel one day as she was eating and was shocked to see a design on her upper back which looked like wings, she also has a little goatee, like the pharaohs in Egypt, which the vets could not explain. Although I call Angel -YoYo sometimes and she has a face shaped like YoYo's, she doesn't look exactly like her. Could it be the same soul in a different body style...creating a different personality? Angel does have *some* of her traits because she's half Siamese just like YoYo was, but she looks more like YoYo's brother Tabby. YoYo was actually half Siamese and half tabby. I love them all. Angel could never replace them, but it makes me happy just to look at her. Then I remember what nice, loving companions they were for all these years and hopefully learn to bless them and let them go, so I can *move forward.*

God: "Be *resilient*!"

I wish there was an animal movie I could watch, something pretty, calm and loving rather than the violent animal movies that are now on TV. I think we have the idea that they have to eat. Now could you stop showing them chewing on one another. First put up on the screen, "This movie contains *no murder*!!" This should apply to your children's movies also. Dameon loves to watch them kill each other.

God: "Please open your eyes. Don't hide anymore for your children's sake and your pets' sake, some people are too old to learn new tricks. *Show* self-esteem and respect *everything. Do something* for a change. How dare you leave it up to the few that are doing *your* job. Help, don't just talk about it, *do* something about it. Talk *is* cheap. Put your money where your soul is, put your time where *your* soul is. *This* is *the real world.*"

Donna with God: "Our goal is to get all the children off of the streets in the United States of America, and get help for all of the stray cats in *the United States.* Then and *only then* can we help the rest of the world. How many people out there know someone who's feeding stray cats? Maybe you are yourself."

A friend from church, Jason, called me today with a message that came to him when he was at a prayer group. You usually say out loud what you would like to pray for. He said nothing at the previous prayer groups. What came to him first was to pray for Donna for help for all cats. Then he finally spoke out for himself and prayed for what he had *never* asked for before; job, health, etc.

God: "He did something *unselfish.* And is being rewarded."

Just as Jason was leaving, four of the five people asked him if Donna wanted their cats, that was a total of seventeen cats! One person had eleven homeless cats, which she had rescued. She was looking for good homes for them. What would I do with seventeen cats? I said, "Have them give me a call." I'm praying they find help. Jason was surprised at the amount of people who needed help with cats. I wasn't surprised at the amount of people who *didn't* offer to *help me.* Did one person say, "I will donate some time," or another, "I will donate money." *No*, they just take! "Will you do *this* for *me?* Will you do *that* for *me*?" Where I come from that's called *using* someone. And *I will not be used*!!! As *you* should not.

God: "I command *you all* to do *my* work here. You *will do whatever* it takes to clean up this universe! The cats *are* my children, the trees *are* my children. Don't abuse them, help them. *I said help them!!!* Are all these poor cats' *lessons to us in vain*?!?"

Donna and God: "There are a lot more cats than you realize that need *our* help! All stores should be responsible in A HUMANE way for any animal on their property, including stray cats; make it a law! When I go to the pet food section in a lot of stores, I smell soap. I wish they would keep the smelly soaps far away from animals food products because the closer it is, the more it penetrates through the packaging, even the cans. The cats, more than dogs, will not eat it and their owners, who don't know any better, will try to force them to eat it by leaving it there for days, which IS cruelty to animals. The stray cats might eat it rather than starve to death. I talk to people in the pet food section who, although they have very *little* money to spare and who are only on social security, are buying cat food for stray cats and kittens. It breaks my heart. It should break yours, too. But where is your heart? No, it's not in yourself. You don't have a heart if you can know about that or see that and do nothing. *We need groups of dedicated people to save them. We* all have problems and the people who are helping the strays have problems, also. Maybe it makes them feel better knowing they are doing *something* to help and as a result are that much *closer to God.* Whatever it is, it's *something* and they can sleep a little better at night. No, the cats are not going away if you stop feeding them. They will just *starve to death.* Would you leave your home if you had no food, or money to buy it? Homeless cats seem to be a little more intelligent, street smart, more appreciative, and more aware than home cats. They obviously *had* to be to survive dogs, raccoons, etc., and the most dangerous animal of all, humans. The first time they come over to you and trust you enough to sit on your lap, they will own your heart. Adopt from shelters. At about age *seven months,* kittens can start *having* kittens, *about* every six months. Sad, please help. I just humanely trapped a black and white cat that I had been feeding for a few months. The first thing I did was make a vet's appointment and I asked the vet if it were a male or a female. If it was a female that was nursing, I would have to find the kittens right away or put her back. The kittens have to eat every *three* hours (like a baby, puppy and an elderly pet). Also, the mother cat's milk might not dry up properly and she would die a *very slow, painful death*.

In the humane trap in the day time, we put paper on the bottom, then cover the cage with a light cloth. One should *never* leave it out all night. *That is inhumane.* Also, you might catch something you don't want in the humane trap, such as a skunk! My stray cat, Blackie, turned out to be a male with no leukemia. If he had feline leukemia, the vet would have had to put him to sleep. If he were not an outdoor cat, I could just keep him in the house. If you have other cats without leukemia, you would have to keep them separated, as feline leukemia is extremely contagious to other cats, not humans. Well, Blackie is home again from the vet's. He has no stitches, so I do not have to take him to the vet's again. I am feeding him extra food and water to build up his strength. When I go away, someone else in my building, or from up the street feeds him. Remember, he *depends* on that. I know he's not mad at me because I found a beautiful rock in his dish recently as a thank you. I just put some straw between some pine trees to keep him warm. Two wonderful men donated it to us. Also the small community humane society paid most of the bill *again*. I don't know what I would have done without you all these years. I hope to have donations for you, as well as others from the sale of this book.

God: *"Thanks from the stray cats and God!"*

Please use humane mouse traps, and then bring them far from homes into the woods to give them a fighting chance. There's a new plug in devise that keeps mice and bugs away. I think whoever invented those SHOCK dog collars which stop dogs from barking, should be arrested now. Did you know that when a plane goes overhead they still get ZAPPED as if they were barking? It goes without saying that any loud noise SHOCKS the poor animal for doing NOTHING!! Return it to the store now, but make sure they don't resell it. Please don't throw your pets away. They'll die. They're use to a warm place and food. *That is* really *murder*. Turn in anyone you know who did that or is thinking of doing it. Animals are very healing. They help to lower your blood pressure and calm your nerves. My cat, YoYo, used to divert me, from *me*. When I was depressed, she could get me to laugh. I wish she were here now!

Toxoplasmosis: My friend, who was pregnant, was told by her doctor to get rid of her cats, because of the danger of toxoplasmosis to the fetus. Most infected people and cats get this disease by eating or preparing raw or undercooked meat which is infected. Please understand that you do NOT need to get rid of your kitten or cats if you have children or when you are pregnant. I have a friend who has a baby two months old and a child two years old. When she was pregnant the first time, her husband cleaned the cat box. The second time she wore strong rubber gloves and was careful not to get any of the stools on her. You can also buy disposable cat boxes, and change them using gloves. My friend has three cats and *now* three children and everything and everyone is fine, thank God! One child, who cries at bedtime, is comforted by one of their cats.

I went to another friend's complex to use her pool and to *rest* from this book, rest from helping cats and rest from other things. While I was there, they mentioned all their stray cat problems. Also, a woman who has a nineteen-year-old cat asked me why her cat cried at night. Because she's over one hundred years old and when you all go to bed she's lost, she probably can't see anymore, or smell as well as she used to, or is having trouble going to the bathroom. No, she's not having trouble in the cat box, but you are probably right about the other things. "It makes sense," she said.

I said, "It's time to say good-bye in a loving way." She's had a wonderful life with you, now let her go to a better place. She just came back down to the pool to tell me when she went upstairs her cat went into the cat box. She stood by and listened and heard a little cry that she had never heard before, because she *never listened* before. She never *learned* before today, she *never looked,* and was not *aware before*. We need to teach basic common sense in dealing with animals in our schools.

God: "Apply *that* to *life with God*."

Donna: "My mother used to say, 'There is *no* rest for the weary.' That's what just came to me, after all these years of not hearing that saying. Now *I know* how my mother felt. Also, when someone lied to her, she said, 'Oh, is *that* it!' *That* took me years to figure out. There's such a wealth of knowledge in older people."

God: "*Embrace it*."

Anyway, I had told the woman with the nineteen-year-old cat, the story about having to put YoYo to sleep and about a friend whom I hadn't spoken to in months calling me and asking how YoYo was. My friend had a realist dream where YoYo was sitting on his window sill washing her left front leg looking content and happy. That was the leg the doctor put the needle in to put her to sleep. Tears came to her eyes and she said, "YoYo was letting you know she was now all right!!!" She now knows what she has to do for her loving companion so she will no longer suffer.

Someone at a "no kill" cat shelter, who lets all the cats out of the cages in the daytime, told me about an older couple who had come in to adopt a cat. The woman was on one side of the room, picking out the cat *she* wanted, while the man, totally disinterested, was standing in the other corner with his arms folded. All of a sudden, a cat reaches out and grabs his arm. He looks at the cat. The cat looks at him. The man says, "Wrap this one up, *we'll take* him home, *too*!!!"

When there's something wrong, a cat will sit and stare in the direction of the problem until someone comes along and *fixes the problem*. For instance, one of my cats had gotten himself closed in a closet. YoYo sat by the door and stared at it, until I opened it and let Tabby out. I noticed Bartet, out on our balcony, staring up at the side of the building. Every time I'd look at her, she would look up and stay in that position like an arrow, or a dog pointing. I didn't go out right away because I was praying it was just a bug passing by. A few minutes later, she was still there, looking at me, then looking up. Looking at me again, then up again, as if to say, "What's taking you so long? You know better! I'm trying to tell you something!" Okay, okay, I'll come out and look. Yellow jackets were forming a nest right by the entrance to my sliding glass door. GROSS, too close. I thought she was so brave to protect her home and me by sitting there all that time. That's what cats do! *You* just have to *learn* what they are trying to tell you. *Cats and other animals SEE much more than we do.* Horses get SPOOKED! Evil people get negative messages channeled *through* dogs. It's funny how cats always go to the person in the room who doesn't like them. After my walk with Dameon/Satan, the stray cat, Blackie, came out from under a bush and just stared at Dameon/Satan. It seemed as if a *very long time* had passed, like a time warp. Blackie looked at me quickly, then steadily stared at Dameon. The stray looked at Dameon just like the cat in a picture of the last supper did. You know, the one next to *Judas*!!!

God's Wish list: We need volunteers of all sorts, large donations, foster homes for children and cats, vans for transportation, humane veterinarians and doctors who will work at a discount, or do some work for free. Maybe we can start an organization which would go to your home when you called with a problem about homeless cats, and possibly other animals, without hurting or killing them. Keep it so that the largest percentage of donated money will be used on the animals, with a very small percentage going to the administrators of the organization. Let's make "no kill" shelters and POUNDS for CATS and do NOT allow them to be taken from any shelter and used in experiments, as they *still* do today. Your lost pet could be next. Let's make the same rules and laws for cats as we have for dogs. January, 1999: Over 500,000 unwanted pets were killed this month. Six million (6,000,000) puppies, dogs, kittens and cats die each year because they're unwanted. NEUTER YOUR PETS!!! Do NOT throw your pets away. Make strict laws to this effect and give awards to people who report those that break the laws. The state insists our *indoor cats* have rabies shots while their *outdoor* cats, living on city, state or federal property, have none. BE HUMANE!!!

Please help the kittens and cats, also adopt from shelters.

Angel

Chapter 26

Fear And Action Is Courage, Come From Behind The Curtain Now

God and Donna: "Please help, please help."

God: "Who cares? You'd better if you want *this* world to exist, one letter away from exit. Remember that. And *no one* can buy his/her way into heaven. *This* is the ticket *showing* you care!"

Donna: "Good thing *we* have brains, huh? If a bird had our brains, he'd fly backwards!!! Let us use our instincts."

God and Donna: "Dolphins, apes, whales, dogs, cats and all other animals have more intelligence than we do. We *are* all one. We *are!!!* Where is your sense of values? Trust me. *Love everything, everything.* You will get your reward *here and on the other side*, for doing *the right thing.* Show that you have character. *Show* your children and friends how you respect *your world.* Don't be afraid anymore. Stand up and be counted. This is where it starts. This is where it has to start or else it will roll downhill to all of us. *Thank God* we have replaced whaling with whale watching. Thanks to the members of GREENPEACE, PETA and many, many other organizations, who have risked their lives to save the whales and seals from that brutal slaughter. See, there *is* a better way, a more God-like existence between God's creatures, the trees and us. Please help! *These loving people* are not hiding, *don't you! Show your* gumption for a change. Show that you *are* king and queen of the mountain."

Toxic chemicals are polluting our oceans as we speak. They are already killing whales and penguins, fish, etc. Right now, *not tomorrow anymore*, it's *right now.* The whales have been here about *twenty million* years. We, humans, have been here only about a million years as far as scientists can determine. Who, other than God, knows the exact number of years? The animals did not disturb *the balance* on this planet in nineteen million years prior to *us*. *We* did it, *we've killed it*. No longer is that statement in the future, it's been going on since yesterday. Why did the government allow pesticides to be used when they were poisoning our waters? Who's going to clean the ocean? What can we do to help close the hole in the Ozone layer? Don't you see *the severity to us? We* have killed our water. We are *all* dead. Save the whales, etc., and you have saved us! Wake up! Please wake up! For the children's sake and your grandchildren's sake. Wake up! It's already too late for some mammals. Our government *gradually* stopped the use of the powerful D.D.T. (Dichloro-Diphenyl-Trichloroethane) in 1972. It affects the nervous system, animal life, and contaminates the food *we* eat. Other parts of the world unfortunately STILL use it. Are we shipping food from there to the United States?? If so how can WE *stop* it? The government knew Dioxon insecticide was a contaminant in 1957, and it was still being used in the mid 1970's, causing death to animals. People were developing stomach aches, skin rashes, birth defects and cancer. There is no organism which can break them down. The government runs a test called LC-50 (meaning lethal concentration) where they trap a certain amount of fish in a tank, if 50% of the fish, or shrimp die in the Dioxon polluted water from MILLS, they consider *that* to be *acceptable*. Acceptable?? Even if the other 50% are so SICK, and disoriented they can *barely* swim after that test. A scientist told me that it's all about *money* and *politics*! A lot of books have been written from the 1960's about how "we are killing ourselves," through the use of pesticides. We're also killing the animals who kill the bugs and insects!

I saw a show on the Discovery channel which said whales and fish are now getting cancer. Why would you want to eat fish after that discovery? I especially would not wish to eat lobster which feeds from the polluted ocean bottom. Next time you eat a stuffed lobster, realize that they are cut open while *still alive*, also baked in the oven while alive, and of course, are thrown, ALIVE into boiling, scalding water for about six minutes, screaming as they slowly boil to death. *What goes around comes around!* I don't think even cavemen would be so cruel. In Genesis they speak of just eating herb-bearing seeds for food. People are using this now and are healthier than they have EVER been, have a lot of energy and also have LOST a lot of weight!

People from earlier times were more respectful of the food they ate, even if it were only a piece of fruit. They thanked their God(s) for his blessings. It isn't necessary to give a long speech to bless your food. Just say, "*Thank you.*"

Getting back to DDT, it's preventing whales from having more calves. On a boat doing research on whales (not hurting them for a change), a couple of scientists were standing on deck, when a mother whale brought her baby next to the boat to show them the serious deformity her offspring had. *It never breaks down.* This brings tears to my eyes. The scientist said it was the typical deformity due to DDT being in the ocean because *it does not break down.* There is *nothing* that can make it break down. Whales are more intelligent than we are, aren't they?!

God: "*Such a cry for help!* Please don't turn your back on their plea or you will ALL be sorry."

Donna: "Is it too late?"

God: "Almost. There would have to be a drastic change. We need dedicated people to change this polluted world."

God and Donna: "We almost lost *our* whales. The fat lady *is* singing! When the whale's song ends, so will ours. They have not destroyed it, *we have*! Now let's get together and clean up our act! This includes ALL countries who abuse this law, and continue to kill whales and seals illegally, and who won't stop their use of D.D.T. Let's use *all* the knowledge we have. Retired people keep busy, keep your hands working, get involved! Get involved with the present and the future. Also, thanks to all the movie stars who have contributed their own precious time and money to the animals. Please keep up the good work! But please tell the writers they're hurting their own children and ours with those awful, dangerous killing movies and savage computer games. Also stop the cat cries!"

God: "*Blood money!*"

God and Donna: "I was watching the Genesis Awards which honors people who work diligently to save animals. I could hardly believe the video about rodeo horses that banged against the tall walls around them to try to kill themselves because of all their sad abuse. *Stop it now! Don't show up* for rodeos, *bullfights* or *circuses with animals*. I saw on the show 'EXTRA' that circus animals were being beaten with long iron rods. *That's not entertainment, that's evil abuse*! Wake up all countries, for God's sake, *wake up!"*

Donna: 1/99: "A woman in Texas is breeding cats whose front legs are a lot shorter than the back legs and are turned in. Picture a kangaroo trying to walk on all fours. These cats have no desire to go outside...they can't defend themselves. Isn't there a law to prevent this abuse to animals? I'm shocked! Please, someone do something before it's too late. Make a new law now. My friend Hank described it as, 'cruel, despicable and horrifying.'"

God and Donna: "I can't even talk about those who hunt with bows and arrows. To me, that is the lowest of low. What could possibly be missing in your life that you would have to, and insist on, making an animal suffer in that inhumane, awful, cruel way? My wish is that you rent the movie, *Powder*, and that you feel the animal's pain, or to reincarnate into a hunted animal. I also wish you 'bluebirds in the spring' and LOVE.

To those who are *still* buying fur: Did you know they pull the pelt from the fox while he's still alive so that they don't ruin the pelt? There *are other* types of coats you could wear that are not as heavy, warm, pretty, and NON-abusive."

God: "*Believe it!* What kind of insensitive world is this? Go away, I can't even understand *this sick* behavior. Don't even try to rationalize *this* to me. It's up to *you* to tell them to *stop*! Yes, your one vote *does* mean something. That one call, that one letter, that one prayer. Don't use their products. TELL them you won't use their product. Don't just <u>not</u> use them, TELL them, TELL them WHY!"

God and Donna: "Sometimes the shows which are supposed to be the "funniest" are the most abusive to animals, children and the elderly. You can also use these videos as a witness to abuse. One video showed a baby being hit on the side of its head (the brain is like jello), and landing across the room. That should be used as evidence. You really put a price on your family and pets. Try using the money to get into heaven. The operative word is, TRY!"

God: "ALL FOR THE ALMIGHTY BUCK! Would someone please tell the hunters there is a supermarket within a couple of miles of where they are shooting? They don't care. Get help."

Donna: "They're illegally hunting ducks in my area. We used to have hundreds of ducks and ducklings in our area. Some rested on our lawns, looking like pretty ceramic statues. I saw only two ducks on our beach last year. The real hunters are even upset with these illegal hunters."

God: "Then why don't *you* do something about them if *they* are *embarrassing you*?"

Donna: "I've been trying to get it to stop for more than ten years. They're shooting in people's back yards, in parks where people walk with their children and pets. They're jolting people from their sleep at 5:00 A.M., way before sunrise which is the legal time to hunt, with loud shotgun blasts when they're supposed to be using air guns. They illegally hunt animals still asleep in their nests, leaving the bodies half dead or rotting. They hunt in places where no one is allowed to hunt. Believe it or not, they can even hunt in certain areas in our Reservation for all birds and animals.

December just before Christmas in 1999, 7 A.M.: I've heard on the radio twice that baby deer have run into traffic on Route 128. What choice did they have, a car or a bullet?

Three people (that we know of) have almost lost their lives within the past few years, due to bullets just missing their heads. One man was walking in the park for *his health*. His doctor suggested walking as therapy after he had a heart attack."

God: "Twice, it was not his time to go."

The hunter, who was there illegally, never went to jail, never received a fine, never got a slap on the hand. It didn't make the media. People called to report this but the media were not interested. *To the press*: Start telling the truth for a change. He was asked not to come back to our area again. The people in town who are supposed to oversee the hunters, *are hunters*. The environmental police hung up on me twice when I called to report the infractions. The first officer was very rude to me.

I calmly asked, "Are you speaking to me this way because I'm a woman?" He hung up on me. I had Hank call him back. Not only was the officer polite to him but took time to describe everything to him in detail. The officer explained hunters were encouraged to also shoot foxes and coyotes because they MIGHT be rabid. Coyotes were living on government property abutting someone's yard and no authority would do anything until a little girl was almost killed by one.

A week later, after I had been awakened again at 5 A.M. by shotgun blasts, I called again. A younger officer yelled angrily at me, saying there were NO environmental police to send to check on the hunters, then he also hung up on me! Maybe they are *trained* to hang up on women and only be respectful to men.

During another call, on December 1998, to the environmental police, the officer said, "The only reason you need to be concerned is if you live by the water, because they're hunting ducks."

I replied, "I DO live by the water, and there are no ducks left. What could they possibly be hunting? "

He said, "So, what do you want to do, go for a walk?"

I said, "Yes," just to prevent another argument about illegal shooting and maiming.

He said, "Wear *bright* orange, and put a *bell* on your pet!"

I said, "But I live in an over-populated area."

He said, "That's OK. Look for posted signs Okaying hunting and be aware. Be VERY aware." (I've never seen one of those signs in my life.)

A lot of *our* politicians *are hunters*. There was a BIG man shown on television last year shooting LITTLE ducks, President Clinton. I guess he doesn't care if *people who love animals* don't vote for him in the next election.

God: "No wonder nothing ever gets done!"

Donna: "I was telling the story about the man walking in the woods, who was almost shot. The man I was talking to became enraged because the hunter was a friend of his. 'We were together that day, they treated *him* unfairly,' he said. Even though we were in his business office, he was pointing his finger at me and yelling at the top of his lungs. I said, 'A man almost died.' He said, I don't care. He didn't die and we should be able to hunt WHEREVER we want to.' (What color is the sky where he comes from, pitch black with bright sparks?) He asked me for my phone number. I respectfully declined saying, 'I don't give my number to hunters.' I was probably giving up a nice dinner and movie (ha, ha) or perhaps avoiding a threatening phone call. How do people like him get guns anyway? Someone there told me he's married. I can only imagine what it must be like for his wife to live with him! Certain hunters have been known to threaten *women* who have questioned their hunting activities but when a man answers, the hunter hangs up.

I have spoken to a few hunters and they've said, 'It doesn't seem like SPORT. They instantly added that they don't hunt like that.'

Dameon told me to say the next time I meet a hunter, 'I want to know what type of gun the animal had. Was *it a fair fight*? I just want to know, *was it a fair fight*?' "

God: "This is not a hundred years ago. I just thought I would let them know that."

Donna: "Let's give the animals birth control if they are *over*populated, as they do for cockroaches and gorillas. Let certain hunters stalk *other hunters* with paint pellets. Maybe if there are overpopulation and illnesses, let's talk. Hear us out and let us find a grey area. Is it a law that all hunters as well as gun owners are to take tests with the National Rifle Association with approved instructors? In other words, if you're going to shoot at an animal, make sure you don't just wing it giving it more trauma than it is already going through. People in my area have brought wounded animals to the vet due to poor shots and paid for the appointment with their own money. Now they want to lower the hunting age. Do you really want *children* to have guns?? God help us!"

God: "I love you, love me! And my creatures!!!"

Donna: "I have a story about a hunter I would like to share with you. This man would just as soon throw you under a bus as look at you and I am NOT kidding about that. Well, it seems he bought about seventy-five acres of land on which to build a house. While walking around his new property, he noticed a deer, who immediately froze. They looked at each other, just stood there staring at each other, with no guns, just the beauty of *his* new woods and this great living breathing animal, standing close to him in peace. I automatically thought he was going to run home, get his rifle and shoot it. But something happened to *him* in *that moment in time*. There was a deer on *his* property. As my father always said, 'We only borrow property.' His home was going to be *there, also*. He said, '*No one* is *ever* going to come on *our* land and kill you. *I'll protect you.*' He now protects *all* the animals on his land and has not picked up a gun since. He has posted 'No hunting' signs everywhere. Also, while walking his land, he was *very lucky* because he avoided stepping into several leg traps which others had placed on his property. You know, those ugly large iron jawed traps which lay open, hidden, waiting for an unsuspecting pet, child or yourself to come along and accidentally step into it. Then it closes around your leg with a fast, hard, ragged tooth-shaped snap. When caught in this type of trap, most animals will gnaw their legs off to free themselves. Fireman are very concerned about accidentally stepping into one. Yes, they are still here and they are still legal even though some humane people spend their own time and money to try to make them illegal. They have made this attempt for many years, to no avail! (Our politicians are hunters.) Men leave these traps hidden under branches and leaves, near streams and in the water. Many times they don't go back for weeks or *never* go back to check them to see what might be caught in the evil trap, leaving the animal to suffer and die a slow and lingering death. This is a very cowardly, sad and sick thing to do."

God: "What type of cruel joke is this?"

In 1995, this article appeared in a local newspaper:

'Barbaric traps' return to Massachusetts

"On June 20, the Massachusetts Supreme Judicial Court declared that the padded leg-hold trap is not subject to restrictions under Section 80A of the Mass. General Law, Chapter 131, enacted in 1974 and so, after 24 years, land-trapping will be allowed in the fall!

The Division of Fisheries and Wildlife supports the use of leg-hold traps, in forceful testimony through the years, though scientific data shows that leg-hold traps, padded or unpadded, are inherently cruel devices.

Unbelievably, we now go backwards, thanks to the division and the hard-hearted decision of the Supreme Court, and we return to the barbaric traps again!

So, those of you who live near woods, fields, streams, or, if in a country setting, guard your small children and pets! The leg-holds will be back in land-trapping season again!

And a warning. Be advised that unless you post your land, the presumption is that traps can be set on it!"

Written by: Althea Griffin of the South Shore Humane Society.

I am thrilled to write November 5, 1996, a law was passed that was purposed by an "initiative petition." Many people worked very hard on their own time to get signatures to change the hunting and trapping laws. Also, the law prohibits the pursuit or hunting of bear or bobcat with the aid of abusive packs of dogs, which is called hounding, and eliminates some restrictions on who may serve on the Fisheries and Wildlife Board.

Section 1: In order to protect people, domestic animals and wildlife from the cruel traps and to facilitate the release of non-targeted animals, the existing language of MASS. GEN. LAWS CH 131, 80A, shall be deleted and replaced with the following provisions: 80A: use of leg-hold traps and other devices restricted.

God's UNIVERSAL mind has struck again!!!

Some hunters went on a hunting rampage. Now they are complaining because there are no more ducks and squirrels around to shoot for sport. They shot them all. Remember there is no actual supervision over hunting activities.

God: “We and our animals won! We are on a winning streak. Now let’s enforce this new law so that the work of all these good people was not in vain. If you see or hear of any wrongdoing, make that call. Show courage, come from behind the curtain now.”

Donna: “The bad news is, 1998, the hunters are trying to bring back the leg traps...Let us pray.

The good news is, the two hunters from Boston, who put the leg traps on that gentleman’s property, came back with a truck full of twenty leg-traps. They were picked up by the New Hampshire police. One was brought to the hospital, apparently he had accidentally fallen into one of his own traps. Then they both were fined for each trap, and are now serving time in jail. Great work officers!!!”

This isn’t about not having guns for protection (out of children’s reach). That to me is a personal choice. A crook on TV said they would never rob a home in Miami because when you ring a doorbell the person living there doesn’t answer the door. Then when you walk through the door, they shoot you. “All’s fair in love and war,” comes to me.

***

Talking about courage: The one good thing about Clinton is he has made a vegetarian burger very popular which took money from the pockets of the meat industry. He has "boca burgers" delivered to the White House by the case. They are high in protein, no cholesterol, fat free, ninety-seven calories. They look like a hamburger but there is *no meat* in them. *They are very tasty.* 1/99: They’re so popular now that the White House no longer has them delivered. They buy them at the local store. I wonder if the next President will use them? A fast food restaurant, which shall remain nameless, is cutting down our rain forest to make room for more cattle. I also understand the cattle are being abused even before they are brutally killed. Can't they do anything right? Life is stressful enough. I don't eat anything that is abused or traumatized on its way to being my food. Genesis 1:29; And God said, Behold, I have given you every herb bearing seed, which *is* upon the face of all the earth, and every tree, in which *is* the fruit of a tree yielding seed; to you it shall be for meat. This was taken from the King James version of the Bible.

God: "Remember *you're* the adult. Your child does not know enough to not eat that greasy food or drink all that tonic. If someone or something is abused, they or it become unhappy, which in turn makes their bodies sick and unhealthy. Teach this to your children."

Donna: "The last time I ate at one of those places, I was sick *all* night and that WAS the LAST time I ate there. Let's start a *clean, fun, healthy and happy* fast food restaurant that doesn't hurt anything and, in turn, anybody. I am not saying take away my onion rings and French fries (once in a while is okay). Let's just take away the abuse and sickness. *Thank you, God*! Also, scientists in the name of science are spraying poison into trees in the rain forest unjustly killing everything in the tree. Even the beautiful butterflies are dying. What happens to the poison the next time it rains?

Remember to watch *your* children around animals and *be aware*. Make sure they're not abusing animals in school yards, your homes, or anyplace else. It's not cute or funny, there's a serious problem. I know three teachers who have rescued animals from being beaten to death in their school yards by children. Do you know where your children are or what they are doing?"

God and Donna: "What's next? Other children? Then adults? Don't be afraid of losing their love by telling them *no*. Or to *stop it! You* are asking for trouble. *You* will lose their respect, then them. Remember, *you* are guilty if they *kill something* or *abuse someone*. Help the animals also, or else, wake up, wake up, dear God, wake up! You can't teach an old dog new tricks, so start with the young. Find help, it's out there. *Show* children you have good character, they *will respect you more*. Tell them, '*No*.' They will love and respect you more. *I* know it's in you. *Now is the time to bring it out*."

Donna and God: "I *love* going out on boats, I love seeing the clouds in the sky and all the beautiful stars, the moon, and sometimes whales."

God: "Their mountainous splashes are *my* fireworks!"

Donna and God: "I wish there were no more lobster pots. The Old Testament says not to eat lobster. I want no more people to throw things off of boats, especially cigarettes and plastic. Pollution is abusive and *it has to stop*. Somehow make laws which set very stiff fines, then back them up, then *make the call* to tell authorities about the abusers. Is there a way of giving rewards HERE for being helpful, besides saying 'you *will* receive your reward in heaven?' We are killing our universe. We have already killed our water. For our sake and for your children and grandchildren's sake, help. We are dying. Help *me*, help."

Donna: "What can we do?"

God: "Stop it, stop it now! *Be aware!* If you know someone doing these things, tell them how you feel in a nice way. *Don't back down! You are right!*"

If you don't want to do that, call a humane society and/or PETA . You don't have to give your name if you choose not to do so. Or write a letter. *We will all unite, the hour has come!!!*

A lot of humane people worked very hard in Boston to get a law passed so the horses that pull carts no longer would have to pull carts in the extreme cold or heat with no medical care and no rest. The horses work too many days and hours a week. *Who enforces it?* Do you call when you see abuse? *Do your* part. The rich can give money and time if they so choose. The poor can give time. No more excuses. No more passing the buck! Please put your money and time where your heart is. *This is it!* Never say the words fear or fail. We will help each other. We will all do our part, one day at a time, to clean up *our world*. Courage.

Say this prayer for problems:

"God, please help me
to resolve this problem
in a loving way."

Also I would like to share this prayer which has helped me a lot. My girlfriend, Glen, received this anonymously through the mail. The source is unknown. The letter said to face north and repeat this saying three times at night, for seven nights. After a couple of nights of not saying it I felt a loss, so now I repeat it often, day and/or night:

"Oh, Great Spirit,
have mercy on me.
I need your help!"

Use your brain, as well as your heart's intuition (which is usually your angel speaking to you), with people who are *trying* to use you. If something negative happens to you today, do you stop and think, "What did I do or say earlier to create this awful thing that has happened to me?" The negative things you say over and over and over, whatever they are, whether it's gossip or even just thinking how much you hate someone or something, it all shows through you and emanates around you, did you know that? Your whole body language, and the expression on your face, things you say and subconsciously do to a person or an event will display the negativity you feel. Whether they live in your house or in another state, they know through the thoughts and psychic vibrations you send out like a universal psychic telephone, that you don't like them. Did you ever have an occasion when you didn't want to go someplace? Then got sick and liked all the loving attention you received, plus you had an excuse not to go out? Did you especially like not having to go to work, so not only did you stay sick, you created more illness? Then do you say, "Why me? Why do these awful things keep happening to me, over and over? What did I do to deserve this?" Once you're *awake*, you won't have to keep asking that question because you'll remember what you said or did to create it. I have been driving down the expressway and been cut off and about a half mile up the road I have seen that person get cut off to the point where they were almost run off the road into the woods or into another car. It was a lot worse than what they had done to me. That's a perfect example of what goes around comes around, the universe mirroring back onto you.

Prayer:

Please, God, teach me to be a better person
and learn to love myself
and in return love others.
I love myself, I love myself, I love myself.
Let go, let God light.

(Mean it when you say it. Now say it again.)

God and Donna: "*This is reality.* You have choices to make in life. The Holy Spirit cannot *make* you take care of yourself. You have to love yourself to do that. A lot of people say, Why does God do this to me? Why does my family do this to me? Why do people do it to themselves? Why do *you* do *it to yourself?* Remember, *God is very tired of taking the blame* for what *you* have done to yourself in this world. You pray hard one day for something, then when you receive your wish, you conveniently forget who gave it to you. You end up doing whatever you want. You think bad thoughts of your neighbor, get drunk, or abuse whoever or whatever. When something negative happens to you that *you* have invited in such as Satan, evil, lack of respect and lack of love, then *you* blame it on God? You don't need a rabbit's foot (it made me sick when I found out as a child they were real) or a horse shoe. *You have to trust in yourself.* It's all in there, you just have to *pray for it* and bring it out *and trust it.* Your luck will change for the better. Don't let *anyone* pull your *power* or take *your power* away from you. They will *drain* you and when they walk away from you, they will feel more powerful because they have taken *your* power. *Don't let anyone question your abilities. Don't let ANYONE EVER question your abilities.* We don't need family or strangers ridiculing us. We do it enough to ourselves. We should *not* do that. We are our own punching bags. So here is your lesson: *We need respect,* we *demand* respect. We need more compassion. We need to be more *grounded.* We need *no more anger*.

Don't try to make me feel stupid, it won't work. *It won't work anymore*! Those are *your* issues, *not mine*! And if you lose someone because you are *awake* now, they were not worth keeping. Say a prayer, white light and pray for them and yourself and then send them away from you *in love*. Say good-bye to fears starting and beginning with childhood. *Laugh* at them, *laugh at them* and get rid of them *now*. Say I am *not afraid* anymore. I love you."

As I was looking over the book *again*, I kept playing the same CD, number seven out of a package of ten CDs, for hours, something I have *never* done before. I looked at the label to find that I had been listening to Symphony No. 9 "From the New World," by Dvorak.

As I am typing, I am getting very sharp pains in my back and distended stomach, the type where I have to lie on the floor. My prayer this time was *not* a happy one. How could someone who works so hard for *you* be in such pain?

God: "You are angry at what *you* create."

Donna: "I feel *so defeated* and was being so Irish, English, Taurus, *stubborn* that I had to get away from this for a night."

God: "You have to be *defeated* to really learn and clear your lessons."

Donna: "I have worked so hard. *Why*???"

God: "You have to teach yourself and know how *you* cleansed to help others cleanse. You did something to create *it,* something *somewhere* in your life to hurt someone or yourself today? Look back in *your* memory and childhood first to see if you carry that, or something into adulthood."

Donna: "After I calmed down and stopped feeling sorry for myself, I looked at some thoughts that have been poisoning my mind *slowly* this past month that I did not even realize *until now.* The first thing that popped into my mind was the first apartment I lived in when I was born. All of a sudden, I was standing *alone* by the front door. I felt sad. Secondly, it's September and the awful memories of going back to school from childhood were in me. In addition, the flowers are dying along with the leaves. The *chill* in the now shorter days seeps into our bones, making us want to stay in bed later. Then there is an awful feeling of the body changing with the temperature *forcing* us to turn on the artificial heat. Also realizing, since childhood that there is more to Halloween, which was quickly coming upon us, than meets the eye. My father and my best friend passed over around this time a week apart, just five years ago and my mother is nearing her move to a better address. I guess *He* was right.

Now, a year later, after going to seven hospitals and two clinics to no avail, I have since learned to cleanse my body and have started a book on my sickness and my healing. I didn't allow September and October to disrupt my life this year."

1/99: I look and feel a lot better. I no longer look seven months pregnant. I am still aware of how September used to treat me and being aware I can now protect myself from those feelings. If I hadn't pulled those muscles in my back and stomach (after working sixty hours that week), forcing me to stay home, I wouldn't have created this and other books and poems with God.

God: "If *we* worried as much about *this world* and *our own true happiness* as *you* do about *your* weight, wrinkles and money, there would be *no* problems ever again in this life or your children's lives or your grandchildren's lives. *Get it?* And stop spending your hard earned money on *evil people's* movies, books, records, etc. They will respect *us* or we will *not* have them in our homes and *we will stop* buying *them* newer and bigger homes. Then *they will listen to us* for a change! *Believe it! Now!* Your priorities are really mindless, *really.* Where is your *respect for yourself?* How *unhappy* could one person be *with himself*? Imagine *yourself* in this world *alone*. Who would you *need* to impress? Let's have a 'good person' contest instead of a beauty contest. Do a good deed, visit a nursing home. Maybe if you did something good for someone or something else for a change, 'with no strings attached', you would *feel* good enough about yourself to maybe automatically lose a little weight. If you have ever met a true spiritual person, you would notice they usually look younger than they are. Their eyes are always glowing and they are usually very busy people. Or, just maybe, you would be *so happy* about *yourself,* for a change, that you would just be happy with *you* ... the way *you are* ... *who you are!"* - ***God***

"I am surrounded in God's light,
I deserve blue skies all day, and sparkling stars at night."

Love erases all fear!!! Love is more powerful than hate! *Happiness is more powerful* than sadness and confusion! If you pray towards the moon and the stars above, *I'll* be there for you! - ***God***

Thank you for such a beautiful day today, God!

God and Donna: "Contributions from this book after our expenses are for young children in the streets of the United States of America and animals, starting with stray cats. If you don't want to give time, give money. If you don't want to give money, give time. Do it for both causes. Leave these causes in your wills.

You will ask, 'How can I help this universe, besides recycling (apartment, condo buildings and businesses)?'

God will answer, 'What can you do?' He will have a wish list. Everything and everybody is on it and needed *now*. From cleaning houses to lawyers."

Help, we are dying!!!

God: *"I am here love, come to me. I love you."*

We are all part of the United States of America and we are all proud to be here. But the fat lady *is* singing. Help! When the USA is strong, then we can go to the rest of the world and help them to help themselves. *No more games. No more shootings, no more drugs, no more hate, no more lies, no more telling stories of you and me.* 1-4-3, I love you. *Just love!* Fear and action does equal courage. Come from behind the curtains of your homes and souls now. 1-4-3, *we* love you! We *are* one, *I* love you. *Love me. And love yourselves*, here and now and forever. (A song just came to me) Love one another. **God.**

Chapter 27

Home To Love And God

"I *hate* me." (A little voice deep within me said.)

Donna: "*Oh, God*, here we go again. Why?"

(?) "Cause (sounded like a child)."

Donna: "Cause why? (I see a *light in me now*.)"

(?) "Cause I don't know how to do that."

The little girl in me never learned.

I love you.

God: "Children unite and be strong. Open up and listen. Here *we are* to show you how. *Trust* in God, white light your souls so no evil can come in. The white light of God and the universe *is us*. Help to protect us from evil and lies."

As we cry, we must laugh! 1-4-3, I love you.

Home, and outside and at work, tell five people a day that you love them then *feel* how *that feels* to *you* inside. Then look in a mirror every day and say, "I love you." *I love you.* Do it now *and mean it*. That's homework. And if you are *not* doing that, you are *not* keeping the commandments.

God: "Going in circles looking for your heritage, *home*."

Donna: "Mine *was* Ireland and England. My true *home* is within *my own soul now*. I have found it. As I pray you do."

God: "Please don't blame *anyone* else for *your disappointment,* for the way *we treat ourselves*. So *don't hate* yourself and others. Hate creates sickness and disappointments to you and then others around you. *So love one another!*"

Donna: "Thank you from us all."

God: "Irish Catholics everywhere pray very deep prayers for their children."

Donna: "I *am* very grateful that *my* mother was Irish Catholic. She prayed for me every day, mostly to Mother Mary."

God: "And because *you all* pray a lot, you are *very* connected to us. The Holy Spirit shows itself to you. Don't deny it. It is in the Bible. Don't think you are going against the Bible. This is part of your learning process *from* praying so much. The things you see *from* the other side *are* real. Trust them, don't deny them. *If they come in love, love."*

Donna: "This is not to take away from everyone else who prays hard every day."

God and Donna: "Where did *all* these religions come from?"

Everyone searching, searching for love in all the wrong places. We are *all* under the same roof. We *are all the same religion*. We are all the same, *we are all the same*. That's why if you hate yourself, you hate your neighbor. If you hate your neighbor, you hate yourself. *We all have the same parents!* Who are all these people *saying they* are holy, yet are *just* asking for money? Ninety percent asking for money, *only* ten percent praying. What's up? Are they giving something to the poor, to charity or back to the people instead of taking from them? Our books are open. What's going on in this crazy world? It's crazy! *You* are only hurting *you*! *I* overheard a few people speaking who go to church every week. What church do *you* go to? And who do you like? And they *judged* people that fell in love and married people of different nationalities and they *judged* their neighbors and they *judged* people who had abortions and they *judged* their friends and they *judged* their own parents and they *judged* divorce. It's a sin. It's one thing to question in a learning way, it's another to judge. People join religions to suit their own purposes. There's actually a religion that uses God's name to do strict things. They are 'closet haters' and unwholesome. They think clean fun is a sin. What bad karma (future hate) are they creating for themselves? *Who* is in *their* closet and now *their children's closets*? *Apparently,* they went to church and *became God*!

Love your faults, then learn from them. Then get rid of them. Embrace them *now! And tomorrow be free.* 1-4-3, I love you. Love your neighbors as yourself. If you are not yet strong enough, or open enough spiritually, it might be better for you to stay away from negative people for now and learn more until *you* are strong enough to be around them. Find or pray for a person who will help teach you further. Please be careful to define greedy, evil individuals from true, channelers from God. God-like people need money also to live. Pray, then listen to your own soul. *We will answer.* To be a healer, you have to look into someone's eyes and soul, to see who they *really* are. Then tell them their lessons and give them the will to live, but it is their choice. We have opened you up a lot tonight. *Learn and live now."*

Donna: "Is God a woman?"

God: "Who is *God* in *your home?"*

God: "Sex."

Donna: "Oh, God, no."

God from young to old: "Why do something with someone you don't know, or love. Get *that feeling of forever and friend and love.* And want to be *with tomorrow and tomorrow.* AIDS is a wake-up call! Hello, hello. Anybody *home*, really home? Herpes didn't work so what's next? PRAY!

Everyone is welcome under this roof. Watch your back until you *know* who the person is behind you. Are you awake spiritually? No guarantees, save yourself now, 1-4-3.

People will see your light and follow you the good way."

God: "Love light is here, around you and *in you.* Pray for it and you will *see it!* Pray deep enough and you will *have it.*"

Donna: "Wow!"

God: *"It is everything, it is God, it is here for you. It is now! I love you now, I love you forever. Please love yourself now! 1-4-3!"*

Donna: "Let's *laugh*, please!"

"Hi! This is me."

Donna: "Who's me?"

"You."

Donna: "What's going on?"

"I'm going to be happy with you."

Donna: "Be more clear. I don't like this joke."

"I'm sorry. Help yourself to laugh."

Donna: "How?"

"Be careful not to stay where you are unhappy. Lighten up."

Donna: "I love when someone says that and doesn't *help* or tell you how?"

"Sorry. You know how. I told you."

Donna: "Me?"

"There is more. Feel, or see it, smell it, be with and taste it now."

Donna: "I don't! I want to! I want to be *it - happy now."*

God: "Thank you!"

Donna: "Me?"

God: "Smell the flowers and trees. Hold a child who *needs it*!!! Or an animal who *needs it*! *They* will end up *healing you. Feel yourself happy and joyful, not sad and sick with hate. Taste* yourself being happy, *share your food* with *someone* who needs it, even if it is just a sad friend. *But be happy!* 1-4-3. *Then* you *all* will be happy. Relax and get *home.* Home to love yourself and be happy. *Love.*"

Donna: "For *once in my life I want* to be perfect and healthy and have the money to support myself. I *need* security, for *once* in my life. *And no pain from now and forever.* For the most part our mothers depended on men. I am *not* going to hang on a cross to get your point across."

God: "You don't *have* to."

Donna: "*Great, thanks.* What then?"

God: "*Sorry* for everyone."

Donna: "I've had enough sorrow. I *command* that I give the word in a great way with *dignity* this time. *I love myself now.* You *will not* treat me like that."

(To everyone from Donna: "This last part was difficult for *me* to write but *I felt the power.* Remember the words for Donna were also being channeled.")

God: "Okay. You shall have what you want." Then there was a very long silence.

Donna: "Nervously laughing, 'Oh, oh, what is *He* up to?' *He is me!!! God* came into me and so has *Mother Mary and Mother Teresa!"*

God: "*Everyone* get off the cross and respect yourselves and *be God-like."*

"The light is us."

Donna: "That's what I saw, the light. The Light of My Life - only for *the God-like*, the *good God!"*

Thank you, 1-4-3. I get *it* now.

Let's create some *good God-like people* now. *Here* and now. Love yourselves and respect yourselves. Get *it* through your heads, use your heads and love one another. *Teach this* to your children, and learn for yourselves. *No more hate!!!* Take *care* to be careful on *your journeys.* You will need protection of light around you. People that are *not* awake or enlightened *might* try to harm you, stay clear for now. When negativity comes in a little, *get it out, push* it out with *white light* as soon as possible. Only the good die young and see what *it* is. Angels come back to you and have a good time seeing what you do here, *for over there.* Don't just take, give back. *Give something back.* Don't kill yourself because there is a place to go. The lessons will be tougher on the other side. You might not step into the *white light* of life that travels to the other side for fear of what might happen to you (staying here in spirit is limbo). *Always go to the light!* If you don't immediately see the light, pray to God for it. You will have to be purified before you move up closer to people who *have learned fully and wholly. Don't test God's strength! He* is already *angry and disappointed,* just ask Noah. Enough said. Thank you. Love…

If there are any more disasters, they will be Satan's doing, like Sodom and Gomorrah. Don't look back, you don't want that vision and memory forevermore. People who act evil will *create* evil and disasters. Change the world for the better before it's too late.

The world is changing. Hang on for dear life.
Arm-aged-don.

11. Thou shalt love one another.

ASK AND YOU WILL RECEIVE.

NIRVANA TO YOU ALL

LOVE

In memory of my mother
Mrs. Margaret (Clark) Howard

On the morning my mother was to be buried, a publisher told me he would promote this book. Although he didn't work out, I felt it was a sign my mother was with me and everything would be okay.

WE ARE BOTH WHOLE NOW!!!

At the wake, four of us saw a shadow of her lips, chest and hands moving, You ARE NOT alone, came to me.

At the church, I felt her cold hand on my right arm as my nephew Jackie spoke of warm and funny memories of my father, John Henry, and my mother, Margaret. Thank you Jackie for sharing those touching memories with all of us. The following one touched me the most.

Near the end, when my mother was in the nursing home and her memory of earth was not as good as it used to be, but of family *passed* was quite clear, my nephew helped my mother into her bed for the last time. She turned slowly towards him while gently touching his arm and said, "Thank you, sir. It's been nice knowing you!!!"

Jackie replied sadly, but sincerely, "*Thank you*, Margaret. *It's been nice knowing you too*!!!"

My mother's soul left her very sick vessel October 10th, 1995. On Friday the 13th, the day of her funeral, it was ten degrees warmer than usual, apparently so my mother would have a beautiful send-off and we could go without coats. As I approached the grave I noticed a large beautiful butterfly sitting on a rock next to mom's grave, intently watching us. As I stood close by, staring at her in awe, she decided it was time to go, and took flight in slow motion, as if a part of her did not really want to leave. She eloquently danced, ever so *slowly*, above the tree tops where she hesitated, for what seemed like an eternity, looked back one last time before quickly vanishing out of sight, but NOT out of mind.

Our loss is heaven's gain.
1-4-3

Wishing

Wishing I could have you here
Still lovingly stroking your hair

Wishing I could hold you tight
Far away from the lonely night

Wishing I could love you
And feel your love for me

Wishing I could hear you say
Your love will always be

Wishing you could see my heart
The way it looks at you

Wishing we could still do
The things we used to do

Wishing I had told you
How much you mean to me

Wishing this was just a dream
And I could have you here
The way it used to be.

Till we meet again
Donna Marie Howard
-1995-

Right after my mother passed, Glen told me it was time for me to write a poem, and this one came flowing out of me. I met Glen and her husband John, in an unusual way, *just* before my mother passed. I consider this wonderful couple's caring friendship to be a loving gift from my mother. This poem has since been published in "Where Dawn Lingers" and "Lyrical Heritage," found in the National Library of Poetry.

My full name is Donna Marie Elizabeth Howard.
My nickname is Dawn.

"Donna Marie" came to my two sisters as they were walking with me in their arms to St. Leo's Church, Dorchester, on the way to having me baptized.

"Elizabeth" came to me as I was walking down the aisle of St. Gregory's Church, Dorchester, on the way to being confirmed.

Hank surprised me one day with this information on my names from the Heraldry book of Science of Tracing Names. Thank you Hank for all your input and your kind, thoughtful words. I also did some research and came up with some information from the Oxford Dictionary of Names.

"Donna": meaning Lady and World rule
The Italian meaning of Donna is woman worthy of respect.

"Marie": meaning Mary. In Roman Catholic countries Marie is especially associated with the Virgin Mary.

"Elizabeth": meaning God is perfect and consecrated (meaning dedicated) to the service of God.

"Howard": meaning composed of the elements, huge and strong heart, soul mind, spirit, and protector of the land.

Thank You

God
Mother Mary
Mother Teresa
St. Michael the Archangel
Angels and Saints
and to all our helpers here
and on the other side.

Also thank you everyone for all of your prayers. Thanks to all of the people who have shared my hopes and dreams, accompanied me with my lessons and circles in my darkest hour, *you*, by your actions and love, have helped me to find

The Light of My Life.

My life will truly begin when I move to God's light, *"The Light of My Life."*

Thank you ALL.
LOVE,

Donna Marie Howard
The children and the cats

GOD

YOU WILL NEVER WALK ALONE.

Donna Howard
P. O. Box 294
Burlington, MA
01803